MANA
THE FU

MANAGING THE FUTURE

UNLOCKING 10 OF THE BEST MANAGEMENT BOOKS

Vic Zbar

First published 1995 by VCTA Publishing, an imprint of
MACMILLAN EDUCATION AUSTRALIA PTY LTD
107 Moray Street, South Melbourne 3205

Associated companies and representatives
throughout the world

National Library of Australia
cataloguing in publication data

Zbar, Vic.
    Managing the future : unlocking the 10 best
    management books.

    ISBN 0 7329 3058 8.
    ISBN 0 86859 263 3 (pbk.).

    1. Management. 2. Organisation. I Title.

658

Cover design by Designpoint
Edited by Robert Walker
Typeset in New Baskerville and *Univers* by
Michael Hast Publishing Services, East Kew, Victoria
Printed in Australia by McPherson's Printing Group

CONTENTS

ACKNOWLEDGEMENTS

Once in a while you have what you consider to be a really good idea. But how do you know for sure? When it occurred to me that there was a definite need for this type of introductory organisation and management text, I was fortunate to be surrounded by people who encouraged me in its pursuit. While it is almost inevitable that someone who told me to 'go for it' will be forgotten in this list (and hopefully will not take offence), I want at least to mention the main characters involved. Tony Mackay, Executive Director of the Incorporated Association of Registered Teachers of Victoria (IARTV), has regularly acted as a sounding board for my ideas and was instrumental in getting the project off the ground. Mike Rowland, of National Curriculum Services, threw his organisation's weight behind the book from the start and has been a constant source of encouragement. Susan Watson, from VCTA Publishing, played a critical role not only in keeping me on track (and on time), but also in pointing me towards some of the texts included in this book. Sandra Cormack, National Professional Development Manager of the Australian Human Resources Institute (AHRI), was continually enthusiastic about this work and promoted it to her colleagues. Graham Andrewartha, National President of AHRI, has not only supported my work, but also written the foreword for this book. Robert Walker's sympathetic editing has improved my own drafts immeasurably while keeping the original content intact. And above all, Jan Schapper and Joe Zbar have had to live with all that the process of producing this book entailed – from sitting outside in the back office reading until late at night, to taking the portable computer away during school holidays. They are my most helpful critics and my greatest supporters. It is to them that this book is dedicated.

FOREWORD

By Graham Andrewartha,
National President, Australian Human Resources Institute

We live in an age of rapid and continuous change. Every year managers are confronted with a dazzling array of new organisation and management texts that demand their attention. Most are so busy, however, that they can do little more than skim the contents, and the essential ideas may remain hidden beneath the surface. In *Managing the future*, Vic Zbar has taken 10 of the most important current texts and made them accessible to busy people who have been postponing reading them in full. Vic has provided managers with an entertaining and readable introduction to the thinking of the foremost organisation and management theorists of our time. But *Managing the future* goes further than just summarising the ideas contained in the 10 books covered. It also provides an insight into the significance of each of the books covered, and it stimulates us to read more, if we have not already done so.

The Australian Human Resources Institute (AHRI) is proud to be associated with the publication of *Managing the future*. Identifying and understanding new ideas and approaches is essential to the work of all human resources professionals. In this book, Vic Zbar, who is a member of AHRI's professional development committee in Victoria, has charted most of the significant new ideas of the past five years. I have no doubt that the book will contribute significantly to the personal and professional development of all those working in the human resources field.

INTRODUCTION

This book introduces busy managers to current thinking about organisation and management. It presents the ideas contained in 10 important texts currently influencing public sector and private sector leaders. There are some very significant differences between the 10 authors and their views; but there is also a great deal of congruence. They all convey three key **features of today's corporate world**:
- the globalisation of the market economy
- the importance of knowledge as the main source of value added
- the growing significance of communication and information technology.

In addition, they all discuss the development of three significant **structural features**:
- networks
- self-employment
- team work.

Another common thread is the philosophy of Total Quality Management (TQM) espoused by the late W Edwards Deming. Whether by accident or design, each author has drawn heavily from Deming's 14 points for management (*see* W Edwards Deming: *Out of the crisis: quality, productivity and competitive position*, Cambridge University Press, UK, 1986), which can be summarised as:
- seek to create constancy of purpose focused on improving both product and service
- adopt the new philosophy of TQM in a holistic way
- stop trying to achieve quality through mass inspection and instead build quality directly into the production process
- develop long-term relationships of trust and loyalty with suppliers rather than awarding business purely on the basis of price
- continually seek to improve production and service systems
- train employees on the job
- lead rather than supervise
- replace fear with security

- break down barriers between the different parts of the organisation
- eliminate slogans or other exhortations to work harder or to produce more
- replace quotas (including management by objectives) with real leadership
- promote pride in work and eliminate barriers to such pride
- encourage and support continual education and self-improvement
- entrust the entire workforce with the task of organisational transformation.

While they do have so much in common, each of the 10 books also has its own approach to the emerging challenges of the new millenium. I've selected each one for the unique contribution it makes to current thinking, as summarised in this table:

Text selected (short title)	Reason for selection
Reich R: *The work of nations*	Its analysis of global economic developments and the implications of these for work and workers.
Senge P: *The fifth discipline*	Its focus on systems thinking and the need to see the whole picture as well as its parts.
Osborne D and Gaebler T: *Reinventing government*	Its discussion of the public sector, an area neglected in management texts.
Peters T: *Liberation management*	The richly illustrated outline of how organisational structure is now as important as closeness to the customer.
Limerick D and Cunnington B: *Managing the new organisation*	Its analysis of the impact that the new network approach has for managers and the task of management.
Carlzon J: *Moments of truth*	Its description of how a large national corporation promoted both employee empowerment and a customer focus.
Covey S: *The seven habits of highly effective people*	The focus on the individual and the essential habits that underpin improved personal performance within and beyond the world of work.

Still L: *Where to from here?*	Its analysis of the current position of managerial women and the opportunities that exist for them in the emerging new organisations.
Handy C: *The age of unreason*	Its outline of the upside down thinking that is necessary to meet the challenges of discontinuous change.
Drucker P: *Post-capitalist society*	Its assessment of the impact that post-capitalism will have on society and the nation state, as well as on the economy.

It is important to state right from the start that this book is not a substitute for the texts that it discusses. Nor is it a pop introduction to organisation theory: a means of gaining the authority to speak about books not yet read. Rather, it aims to give the reader a taste of what each of the books has to offer and to encourage a fuller reading of those that capture the imagination.

Think of this book as you would a series of film reviews. It gives you a summary of the plot, it outlines why the work is significant and interesting, and then it points to the best bits.

When you have decided which of the books particularly engages your interest I hope you will go on and read, if not the whole book in each case, at least those chapters nominated as most important.

The discussion of each book uses a common format:
- brief biographical information on the author
- an indication of why this particular book is significant
- a summary of the main ideas espoused in the book
- a sentence on each chapter of the book, with an asterisk indicating which chapters are most significant.

The format allows more than just a summary of each text discussed: it draws out the fundamental arguments of each author.

Each of the 10 books discussed is an important book that deserves to be read in full. This book has been written as an introduction to the basic ideas to get you by until you have the time and energy to read the texts for yourself.

– *Vic Zbar*

1
WORK AND ECONOMICS IN THE TWENTY-FIRST CENTURY

Robert Reich – *The work of nations: preparing ourselves for twenty-first century capitalism*
(Simon and Shuster, 1991, 331 pages)

ABOUT THE AUTHOR

Reich is a highly respected political economist who until recently was a professor at Harvard University's John F. Kennedy School of Government. He is currently the Secretary of Labor in the Clinton administration.

Reich has been a contributing editor to *The New Republic* and a frequent contributor to the *Harvard Business Review* and *The Atlantic*. He is the author and co-author of a number of books including *The next American frontier* and *Minding America's business*.

THE SIGNIFICANCE OF THIS BOOK

Any book written by someone who has the ear of the President of the United States is significant. This significance can only be enhanced when that person is also a member of the US Cabinet (with responsibility for Labor) and has been described by *Time* magazine as 'Clinton's economic ideas man' (23 November 1992). The significance of Reich's book is not, however, purely a product of his personal status: it is also related to the book's content.

In *The work of nations* Reich has sought to dispel a number of myths concerning the national economy. He argues that globalisation has greatly reduced the capacity of nation states for effective political intervention. The implications of this for governments, corporations and individuals are all then discussed.

The work of nations provides a comprehensive outline of what nations must do if their economies are to thrive in an increasingly borderless world.

Sir Charles Villiers, former chairman of British Steel, says that 'Bob Reich lives at the frontier of our understanding of political economy, and in this book he has pushed that frontier further than anyone else ' (back cover).

THE AUTHOR'S BASIC ARGUMENT

Reich's overriding contention is that we are rapidly approaching a genuinely global economy. Money, technology, information and goods cross national borders effortlessly. This globalisation is making the concept of the nation state, not to mention national economies and corporations, irrelevant. 'All that will remain rooted within national borders are the people who comprise a nation' (page 3).

He then expands on this basic contention under four broad headings: the economic nation; the global web; the rise of the symbolic analyst; and the meaning of nation.

THE ECONOMIC NATION

National economies are, according to Reich, a fairly recent phenomenon. Prior to the 18th century wealth was produced for the enrichment of the sovereign, not the wellbeing of the nation's citizenry.

It was the spread of the democratic ideal – most strongly promoted by the emerging group of bankers and merchants who wished to 'secure their property, trade freely, and put an end to aristocratic privilege' (*Reich*, page 15) – that led to a concern for the living standards of the nation's population and, subsequently, the emergence of economic nationalism.

The democratic state elicited stronger bonds of citizen support (patriotism) than the sovereign states which preceded it, and these stronger bonds in turn led to the idea that the nation's economic well being was the responsibility of the entire population. Inevitably there were also varying degrees of government intervention in the national economy to promote economic well being. The most notable example is the introduction of tariff protection, which became the subject of much debate throughout the 19th century, as it still is today.

The productivity revolution of the late 19th century consolidated the trend towards economic nationalism by creating a more competitive world environment.

Reich argues that the rapid expansion in production led to an oversupply of many goods and services and a consequent decline in prices. Manufacturers responded by competing aggressively in the emerging world market, seeking out new markets and protecting their own national markets through tariffs.

As each developed country's market became closed off to its competitors, these nations turned towards the poorer countries as potential markets for the goods they could not sell at home: an approach that came to be known as imperialism. The resultant competition between advanced countries for these so-called backward markets strengthened the win/lose view of economic success and ensured that economic nationalism became firmly rooted in many nations.

However, these approaches to oversupply, including price cutting, failed to deal with the high degree of competition in the domestic market. Such approaches therefore proved to be an inadequate solution to the problem.

Towards the end of the 19th century the high level of internal competition was reduced by a concentration of production in a smaller number of large corporations.

For many, Reich argues, these giant companies came to be viewed as the guardians of the nation's economic interests. Many others however, especially in the US, expressed serious concerns about the power they wielded and the influence they could bring to bear.

This concern manifested itself in numerous demands for the large corporations to be more accountable; and then, from the First World War onwards, in greater government regulation and increased government activity in economic planning.

There was, in particular, a conscious effort to enhance the power of smaller groups in society. In the US, unions were sanctioned and allowed to engage in collective bargaining, while shareholder interests were protected through legislation. The result was that corporation executives, along with the public at large, came to view themselves as stewards of various interests existing in the population.

By the 1950s the world economy was a scene of burgeoning consumerism and mass production. The large corporations were, according to Reich, so significant in this economic boom that corporation interests and the interests of the US nation and its people were seen to be fully interwoven. Charles Wilson caught the flavour of it in his oft-quoted (though apparently inaccurate) aphorism: 'What's good for General Motors is good for the US'. Reich contends that this view has endured up to the present day.

He points to two particularly important aspects of this period:

THE NEW MIDDLE CLASS

There was a major increase in the size of the American middle class. These were people who held most of the new skilled, semi-skilled and clerical jobs and who, on the other hand, caused much of the market growth for the goods that were produced.

The emergence of this large middle group of technicians, supervisors, middle managers and the like blurred the previously sharp divide between those who produced and those who operated the business.

THE NATIONAL BARGAIN

Large corporations became responsible for continued national prosperity. In return, the government accepted responsibility for creating the climate in which the corporations could thrive: overseeing the general state of the economy; providing the education necessary to train the nation's workforce; and ensuring the defense of the realm. This was the 'national bargain' (page 58).

In the favourable economic conditions following the Second World War, the US was still, perhaps ironically, not much of a trading nation, directing most of its production towards its domestic market. America was only really propelled into the world's markets later on when faced by competition from the Soviet

Union. This, according to Reich, worked to the advantage of the large corporations which soon realised that the efforts to spread America's own brand of capitalism and freedom came with increased access to other countries' markets.

Corporations that entered world markets proved to be more effective in extending America's influence than either the Defence Department or the Central Intelligence Agency (CIA).

Inevitably the Europeans too, fearful of becoming mere colonies of the US, joined the race by creating and promoting their own corporate giants to compete on a world scale.

As Reich points out, however, 'Americans were to discover that foreigners could undertake high-volume production of standard goods...and sell them in the US' (page 69). This trend was exacerbated from the 1970s onwards by better technology, cheaper communication and improved transport between nations.

The US was now in the midst of a highly competitive world market. The giant corporations responded with a series of strategies, including:

PROTECTIONISM
Corporations called for a revival of the protectionist measures that had eased while the US was seeking to expand world trade. Domestic protection proved relatively ineffective, however, since the foreign trading competitors were able to focus on the rest of the world at the expense of the US. Protection also raised prices for American products at home.

COST CUTTING
There were efforts to match the competition's price levels by cutting staffing levels and lowering wage rates or even, where necessary, going offshore to produce. These strategies also failed, since the competitors also lowered their prices and profit margins in order to match the US move.

FINANCIAL DEXTERITY
Many large corporations transformed themselves into financial institutions. They acquired assets irrespective of any connection

to their original core business. But, while initial tax advantages may have been substantial, these transactions in the end did nothing to enhance competitiveness and, in most cases, did not increase company earnings. And the underlying problems remained.

Thus, irrespective of the measures adopted, Reich argues that the profitability of America's (and Western Europe's) major corporations declined from the 1960s on. The measures were futile because, according to Reich, they were based on restoring profitability to national corporations at a time when these were 'ceasing to exist in any form that can meaningfully be distinguished from the rest of the global economy' (page 77).

The prime determinant of economic success had become *the ability to sell one's knowledge and skills in the world marketplace*; and the major corporations had failed to realise this.

THE GLOBAL WEB

Today's corporation is a very different creature to that described in the first part of Reich's book. An increasingly decentralised and networked organisation, it is no longer characterised by high volume production of goods and services at a central location. Its identity is transnational rather than national.

Having failed in their attempts to replicate the past, the large corporations, Reich argues, are moving away from high-volume towards high-value production designed to meet the specific needs of the customer. Corporations can now remain profitable by applying knowledge to meet customer demand rather than by trying to compete in the high-volume market with uniform goods and services. These can usually be produced more cheaply somewhere else in the world.

Firms are now starting to rely on a new set of **skills as the source of value**:

- problem solving
- problem identifying: working with customers to identify their needs; and then demonstrating how particular customised products can meet those needs

- facilitating: the skill of brokering solutions by bringing together the right teams of people to do it.

'The three groups that give the new enterprise most of its value … (are) problem solvers, problem identifiers and strategic brokers' (page 87).

The work of these people requires constant contact and most certainly does not lend itself to bureaucratic structures and formal hierarchies.

In the high-value enterprise the old pyramidal structure is therefore giving way to a sort of spider's web where the strategic brokers at the centre link together many parts of a multi-talented network. Reich calls this the new 'enterprise web'.

Since speed and agility in identifying and solving problems are what matters most, the enterprise web avoids building up a large, fixed infrastructure by sub-contracting many routine tasks and leasing space and equipment.

The relatively small number of people who work for the organisation in an ongoing capacity are united by a common vision of what they seek to achieve and by the fact that they share both the risks and the rewards of the enterprise. This tends to encourage a degree of experimentation and risk taking that was unknown in the high-volume enterprises of the past.

The subcontractors who exist at the edge of the web not only supply goods and services more efficiently than would otherwise be possible but, because they are specialists focused on a single task, they are constantly seeking to become even more efficient at what they do.

The **key assets** of the new high-value enterprise are, according to Reich:

- its skill in linking customers' needs to tailor-made solutions
- its reputation for having successfully done this in the past.

Power and leadership in these circumstances are the product of a person's ability to add value to the enterprise, rather than of a particular position or title.

These enterprise webs now have so many people bound up in them, and there is so much contracting out and sharing of risks and rewards, that there is no clear sense of ownership or control about them. The great American (or European) corporation has become a myth. The corporation, Reich says, is just a coordinator.

This is a development that calls into question the national bargain (see above). The rewards to the brokers and the problem identifiers and solvers are taking over from the salaries and profits of labour and capital. Over the last 20 years the share of gross national product (GNP) going to both production workers and profits has declined markedly, while knowledge workers have taken an increasingly larger slice of the cake.

The new global, high-value enterprise webs have, in Reich's view, overtaken national corporations. The concepts of 'national corporation' and 'national product' no longer have meaning. A country's competitive performance is no longer a product of the performance of its major corporations. Rather, a nation's economic performance is more closely associated with the knowledge and skills that its people can bring to various international enterprise webs.

These webs are international partnerships of problem identifiers, problem solvers and strategic brokers. These people contract out standardised, high-volume production to the low-wage countries of the world.

Concern about foreign ownership and control is an increasingly irrelevant issue in this situation, because the skills and insights that actually produce the wealth generally remain in the host country. Reich has a good illustration: when Sony purchased CBS they did not acquire Bruce Springsteen as an employee – Springsteen remained an autonomous individual, contracted to a Japanese-based network and earning at least as much as he ever had before.

Ironically, then, a nation is actually *better* served when foreign interests invest in its people and their skills: better served than when it invests abroad in other countries' people. This is an issue which only the 'power of vestigial thought' (page 154) prevents policy makers from recognising.

Reich feels that knowledge-rich nations should encourage the entry of global enterprise webs into their territory rather than seek to impede attempts at investment from outside.

THE RISE OF THE SYMBOLIC ANALYST

This third section deals with the skills needed by any nation to guarantee national prosperity. The main task, Reich says, is to ensure the workforce is adding sufficient value to the world economy.

Along with global enterprise webs, we are seeing the development of an international labour market where competitiveness relates to the value that people add rather than to the prosperity of national champions. 'Battle lines no longer correspond with national borders' (page 171). There is increasing divergence within nations between those who share in prosperity because of the skills and insights they possess and those who miss out because their contribution is not valued in the global marketplace.

Reich contends that, with the development of an international labour market, the old categories for analysing work no longer apply. We need to develop a new schema to fully appreciate the true competitive position of workers in the world's economy. Reich then identifies three specific **categories of work**:

ROUTINE PRODUCTION SERVICES

These include the activities required for traditional high-volume production. The category is broader than just blue-collar assembly-line work, encompassing as well routine supervisory activities and many information-industry activities such as coding and data entry.

Routine work is usually undertaken by large numbers of people, working in a common location and undertaking virtually identical tasks. It is not highly skilled and is heavily regulated by standard procedures and tight supervision. Remuneration is a product of hours worked or the amount of work performed.

While routine production services still account for a significant proportion of the workforce in countries such as the US and Australia, it is a proportion that is declining markedly.

IN-PERSON SERVICES

As is the case with routine production services, this work is simple, repetitive, not highly skilled, closely monitored, and rewarded according to time served or work performed. The difference between this and routine work is that in-person service is provided directly from one person to another and hence is not marketed and sold on a global scale.

In-person workers, who provide services such as cleaning, child care and secretarial support, usually work on their own or in small teams. Their interpersonal skills are as important as their technical abilities. In-person services now account for a significant proportion of the workforce.

SYMBOLIC/ANALYTIC SERVICES

This kind of work encompasses the problem-identifying, problem-solving and strategic-brokering activities that Reich calls the main source of value added in the last years of the 20th century.

The people providing these services – research scientists, merchant bankers, entertainers, consultants – often work on a global scale, entering into networks and partnerships according to the task they have to fulfil.

Income for the symbolic analysts is determined by the *quality* and *effectiveness* of the activities performed. Thus, their income, unlike the incomes of those paid for time worked or work performed, can be highly variable over the course of their careers.

Symbolic analysts are generally well educated and most certainly highly skilled. They constitute a smaller proportion of the workforce than the other two categories although the proportion has increased markedly over most of the post-war period, with the possible exception of the 1980s.

Reich suggests that these three categories of work together account for about 75 per cent of American jobs, with the remainder comprised of farmers, miners and government employees.

This divergence in types of employment is manifesting itself in a parallel divergence of the 'economic fates of Americans' (page 196). The 1950s and 1960s were, according to Reich, characterised by a growing middle class with a relatively small number of people being considered as either rich or poor. Since the 1970s, however, there has been a gradual hollowing out of this middle group, with a greater number of people achieving substantial wealth through the skills they possess and an even greater number of people being pushed down into poverty as their jobs disappear.

Routine producers are faring badly because their high-volume work can now be undertaken anywhere in the world and hence production is shifting to wherever labour is cheapest. The implications of this for routine producers (including the middle managers who supervise them) are only compounded by the increasing use of technology, such as robots, to undertake many mechanical production tasks.

The picture for in-person servers is less clear. While there appears to be an overall decline in their fortunes, it is occurring less rapidly and the impact on individuals is somewhat uneven. While in-person servers seem to be immune from global competition, they are increasingly having to compete with displaced routine producers and various labour-saving devices: it is now possible, for example, to conduct all of one's financial dealings without ever coming in contact with a bank employee. Reich suggests that the demand for in-person servers will remain high because people have 'an almost insatiable desire for personal attention' (page 217). However, competition will keep wages low.

Symbolic analysts, or most of them, are the real winners in the modern world. As communications and technology continue to progress, the demand for their services also grows. Some of the most highly-remunerated people in the world are American symbolic analysts engaged in advertising, management consulting, public relations and entertainment.

While the world-wide supply of symbolic analysts is increasing, Reich suggests that Americans will continue to be particularly successful because:

- future American symbolic analysts are getting **a better education** than anyone else. While the bulk of the US school population arguably is provided with a 'standardised education designed for a standardised economy' (page 227), 15 to 20 per cent of students, potential symbolic analysts, attend schools where they have state-of-the-art facilities and where formal schooling is supplemented by high levels of parental involvement that provides them with additional cultural experiences and educational materials. These young symbolic analysts are taught the basics, but they also learn about conceptualising and solving problems. According to Reich, the four fundamental skills they learn are abstraction, system thinking, experimentation and collaboration: the bases of problem identifying, problem solving and strategic brokering.

• the US already has a **critical mass of symbolic analysts** in residence. What is more, these people are not so easy to move. Specialised symbolic analysts often congregate in geographic areas, such as film makers and musicians do in Los Angeles. Another LA cannot easily be replicated because, while its pro- ducts can move around the world in seconds, the major players tend to stay where interaction and learning can occur.

THE MEANING OF NATION

In the final section of *The work of nations*, Reich addresses the social dimension. In particular he looks at the growing inequality within Western nations (especially the US) and the inability of individual nations to deal with this.

Reich suggests that options do exist for redressing the growing inequality and that these centre on 'good education, training, health care and public infrastructure' (page 250). However these are costly options and they inevitably raise the question: 'Who will pay?'.

Reich's own view is that the winners in today's world, the symbolic analysts, should pay. But, as he quickly points out, there is likely to be an unwillingness to bear these costs in a world where they, the affluent few, no longer depend for their wellbeing on the rest of the population.

The wealthy symbolic analysts have effectively seceded from the nation. The fortunes of the rich have become more closely associated with global enterprise webs than with their fellow country people. They have, very unfortunately, minimised their tax burden to the point where they spend very little on public programs: they do not invest much in broadening the nation's knowledge or in developing the skills of its workforce. And, to emphasise their secession, they tend to establish well-serviced enclaves that are physically separated from the rest of the population. 'As the top becomes ever more tightly linked to the global economy, it has less of a stake in the performance and potential of its less fortunate compatriots' (page 301).

For Reich this raises the question of whether the concept of citizenship can ever compensate for the fact that people within the one geographic nation no longer operate in the same economy. What he is seeking is not a nationalistic or competitive citizenship that ignores current reality and wishes to take on the world, but a global citizenship that accepts responsibility for the 'world's problems and possibilities' (page 309). His fear is that the global status of the symbolic analysts may lead to a decline in social responsibility and a resistance to any action that involves sacrifice.

By contrast, Reich's hope is that nations may opt for a version of 'positive economic nationalism' whereby the citizens of each nation accept responsibility for both enhancing the productive capacity of their own people and working with other nations to ensure that the benefits can be shared.

THE CHAPTERS

(The more significant chapters are indicated by an asterisk)

Introduction* Provides an overview of the implications of globalisation for the economies and societies of individual nation states.

Chapter 1 Traces the emergence of national economies alongside the spread of democracy in the 18th and 19th centuries.

Chapter 2 Describes how the late 19th century revolution in manufacturing methods contributed to the consolidation of economic nationalism as production expanded and countries competed against each other for markets.

Chapter 3 Discusses the emergence of large corporations within national economies and the developing tendency to identify the national interest with corporate success.

Chapter 4   Examines the growing significance and popular im-
                 age of large corporations in the boom years of the
                 1950s, and charts the emergence of America's large
                 middle class.

Chapter 5   Discusses the 'national bargain' that was instituted
                 whereby the government ensured the appropriate
                 conditions for corporations and the corporations
                 delivered continued economic wellbeing.

Chapter 6   Charts the growth of global competition to the US
                 corporations and the failure of the various strategies
                 adopted to respond to this.

Chapter 7*   Traces the corporate shift away from high volume
                 towards high value production in order to meet the
                 unique needs of customers.

Chapter 8*   Explains how the high value enterprises will be non-
                 hierarchical enterprise webs rather than traditional
                 bureaucracies.

Chapter 9   Explores how the operation of enterprise webs leads
                 to a diffusion of ownership and control.

Chapter 10   Explains how national corporations have given way
                 to global enterprise webs linked by 'electronic blips
                 that move through the atmosphere at the speed of
                 light' (page 111).

Chapter 11   Further charts the decline, if not demise, of the
                 national corporation or, to use Reich's term, 'The
                 National Champion'.

Chapter 12   Completes the discussion of the growing irrelevance
                 of any sense of corporate nationality and ownership
                 in the new global economic environment.

Chapter 13   Examines how 'vestigial thought' leads to inappro-
                 priate policy responses as politicians react to a world
                 that no longer exists.

Chapter 14*   Outlines the three types of jobs that will constitute
                 most of the future international labour market: rou-
                 tine production services, in-person services and sym-
                 bolic analyst services.

Chapter 15   Digresses from the main text to consider how govern-
               ments can structure markets so that the skills of
               symbolic analysts may be used for the good of society.
Chapter 16   Examines US incomes and increasing inequality.
Chapter 17   Suggests reasons for the divergence in incomes and
               relates it to the function that workers perform in the
               world economy.
Chapter 18*   Starts a discussion of the type of education that is best
               suited to the development of symbolic analysts and
               identifies the key skills to be taught: abstraction,
               system thinking, experimentation and collaboration.
Chapter 19   Completes the discussion of the education of sym-
               bolic analysts by considering the learning that occurs
               on the job.
Chapter 20   Argues that in a world where national corporations
               increasingly are irrelevant, there is a need to redress
               the burgeoning inequalities through measures such
               as income tax changes and programs designed to
               enable more people to operate like symbolic analysts.
Chapter 21   Traces the secession of the US symbolic analysts as
               their fortunes become more closely aligned with glo-
               bal enterprise webs than with their fellow Americans.
Chapter 22   Argues that low taxes, low public expenditure and
               low budget deficits are all policies based on 'vestigial
               thought' and are likely to stifle development of the
               nation's knowledge and skills.
Chapter 23   Expands on the earlier theme of secession by explor-
               ing the tendency of symbolic analysts to establish
               enclaves that are physically separate from the rest of
               society.
Chapter 24   Examines why US governments have allowed this
               secession to occur virtually without comment.
Chapter 25   Considers the implications for citizenship and social
               responsibility of a situation where members of the
               same population are no longer part of the same
               economy.

2
SYSTEMS THINKING IN THE LEARNING ORGANISATION

Peter Senge – *The fifth discipline: the art and practice of the learning organisation*
(Random House, 1992, 424 pages)

ABOUT THE AUTHOR

Peter Senge is the Director of the Systems Thinking and Organisational Learning Program at the Sloan School of Management in the Massachusetts Institute of Technology. He has conducted workshops around the world for executives and managers of such corporations as Ford, Digital Equipment, Apple, Procter and Gamble, the AT&T Corporation and Royal Dutch/Shell.

THE SIGNIFICANCE OF THIS BOOK

It is difficult to pick up a recent organisation or management text that does not either refer to, or directly quote from, Peter Senge's *The fifth discipline: the art and practice of the learning organisation.*

The popularity and significance of this book appears to stem from three major factors:

- The growing realisation within business, industry and government that the new information society requires learning organisations characterised by continual development and improvement. The book discusses an idea whose time has clearly come.

- The fact that the outline of the five learning disciplines is accompanied by tools for putting them into practice. In this regard, the book is something of a learning experience in itself. The inclusion of the tools and numerous examples to illustrate their use has resulted in the production of a highly

practical book.
- The importance of the corporations that have effectively been involved in the production of the book. The Centre for Organisational Learning that Senge and his colleagues have established is a consortium of major corporations working in partnership to bring the ideas of the learning organisation into the mainstream of management practice.

In many senses Senge's *Fifth discipline* is a direct descendant of W. Edwards Deming's work on quality management. Deming's management philosophy is essentially about creating learning organisations. It is about promoting an intrinsic motivation for learning rather than merely using extrinsic punishments and rewards. Deming believed that profound knowledge – which includes understanding a system, statistics, a theory of knowledge and psychology – is required for the achievement of quality.

THE AUTHOR'S BASIC ARGUMENT

Put simply, a learning organisation is a group of people continually enhancing their capacity to create what they want to create.

Senge argues that successful organisations in the 21st century will be learning organisations that gain the commitment of all of their people, whilst simultaneously developing their people's capacity to learn.

Senge identifies five disciplines that need to be mastered in order to build these successful learning organisations. In doing so he uses the term 'discipline' much as it is used to cover an area of study such as the humanities, or the sciences. It is something to be studied in an ongoing way so as to continually develop and extend our skills and competencies.

The five disciplines are:

PERSONAL MASTERY

Organisations are really only collections of individuals. Therefore, a learning organisation requires learning individuals. Personal mastery is the discipline which relates to individual learning. In Senge's view it is based on the development and continual clarification of a personal vision – based on what we really want out of our lives – to provide the framework for individual action. The energy source for personal mastery derives from the creative tension that exists between what we truly want (our personal vision) and the current reality – 'holding a vision and concurrently telling the truth about current reality relative to that vision' (*Senge*, page 357).

MENTAL MODELS

These are the frameworks that exist within our mind that determine how we view the world – our assumptions, our prejudices and our predilections. Mental models are the things that lead us to say, 'No, that's not possible' even before we have considered the proposal in depth. This discipline focuses on bringing these mental models to the surface so they can be examined, discussed and challenged. It is in part about envisioning alternative ways of seeing and thinking about the world. When people work with this discipline they expose their own ways of thinking and make them more open to the influence of others.

BUILDING SHARED VISION

The important word in this discipline is 'shared' – to contrast with an individual leader's vision which has been imposed on an organisation. A genuinely shared vision has the capacity to energise and enthuse people. Thus, this discipline is concerned with the development of a vision which people in an organisation are committed to, as opposed to one with which they are merely complying. A truly shared vision leads people to do things because they want to, not because they have to. Since leadership within an organisation involves building a shared vision from the personal visions of its members, it encourages and builds on personal mastery.

TEAM LEARNING

Teams are the basis of learning in the organisations of the 1990s and beyond. Thus, just as individuals must be able to learn, so must teams if organisations are to become learning organisations. There is a tendency to assume that the mere formation of teams will lead to success. It will not. There are many examples of teams that amount to less than the sum of their parts. This discipline aims to promote team success through team learning. This requires dialogue as well as the willingness and capacity of team members to suspend assumptions and engage in genuine thinking together. Discussion and dialogue are necessary for overcoming defensiveness and other patterns of interaction that keep people from learning either individually or as a team. Through team learning the whole can become smarter than the parts.

SYSTEMS THINKING

Systems thinking is a framework and a set of tools that enable us to see beyond the parts to the whole picture, and see the forces and dynamics at play. The book provides several examples of systemic and non-systemic thinking, often drawn from the experiences of major corporations such as Royal Dutch/Shell, Apple and Ford.

One of Senge's central contentions is that we need to see the whole of any issue or problem, and not just focus on its parts. By focusing on the whole – the big picture – we are more likely to see the underlying causes of problems as well as the possible consequences of our actions. And seeing causes and consequences is essential for achieving the outcomes that we actually seek from the actions that we take.

Systems thinking, the 'fifth discipline', brings together the other four listed disciplines and shows how they interact. It constitutes a central point. And it encourages us to see how the organisation and its people relate to the rest of the world.

The five discipline's are, in Senge's view, important tools for overcoming a number of major, interrelated **learning disabilities** in organisations. The seven learning disabilities he identifies are:

I am in my position

This is the tendency to see no further than one's own position in the organisation and to assign blame to others when something goes wrong.

The enemy is out there

This extension of the first disability recognises that we all have the propensity to look for scapegoats rather than address our own (individual and organisational) role in creating problems that occur.

The illusion of taking charge

This occurs when we proactively pursue a course of action without having analysed the real causes of the problem/issue, or the likely consequences of our actions.

The fixation on events

This is the organisational equivalent of the cliché: 'Today's news is tomorrow's fish-and-chips wrapper'. If we focus purely on individual events then we are unlikely to see the longer-term patterns that underpin what has happened.

The parable of the boiled frog

In the same way as the frog of this well-known tale sits in the pot as the heat is slowly increased (until it is unable to climb out and eventually boils), people and organisations will often only respond to sudden and sharp stimulus while ignoring gradual change.

The delusion of learning from experience

While few would argue that we learn best from our own experience, learning disabilities can arise in situations where the consequences of our decisions and actions are so far into the future that they do not necessarily affect us.

The myth of the management team

To avoid the pain of deeply questioning our own behaviour as individuals and team members, we often gloss over, or steamroll disagreement and seek the lowest common denominator. Thus, in spite of the best intentions, in many organisations management teams fall apart and then fail to deliver when the pressure is really on.

All seven learning disabilities are well illustrated in the description of a simulation called *The Beer Game*, which is discussed in detail in Chapter 3 of Senge's book. As noted above, systems thinking is the key to the five disciplines – 'the cornerstone of the learning organisation' (page 55). The other four disciplines, which are discussed in detail in Chapters 9 to 12, contribute to the ability of individuals, teams and organisations to think systemically and then to act on the basis of the understanding that has been gained.

Perhaps the most important of Senge's messages about systems thinking is that *structure influences behaviour*; and he outlines a number of archetypal ways in which this occurs.

Understanding these archetypes (which are discussed in Chapter 6 and detailed in Appendix 2 of the book) enables us to look beyond individual behaviours. Instead we can identify the underlying structure which has caused the problem at hand and influenced the actions of individuals involved.

The task is to seek to understand the larger system within which we operate and our own interrelationship with that system. By gaining such understanding we can then endeavour to identify 'high leverage' actions aimed at changing the patterns of behaviour that we observe.

To assist in this task, Senge provides a number of systems-thinking tools, including systems diagrams. These diagrams are illustrated stories aimed at increasing our understanding of patterns of behaviour that he perceives, such as **circles of causality**.

As an example of a systems diagram showing circles of causality, consider why you have purchased, and are reading, this book. It may be that you wish to increase your understanding of the latest organisational and management thinking.

However, it is unlikely that a reading of a summary text will, in itself, lead to the level of understanding that you desire. Rather, it will influence your behaviour within a particular structure, or pattern of behaviours. This can be represented in the form of a systems diagram:

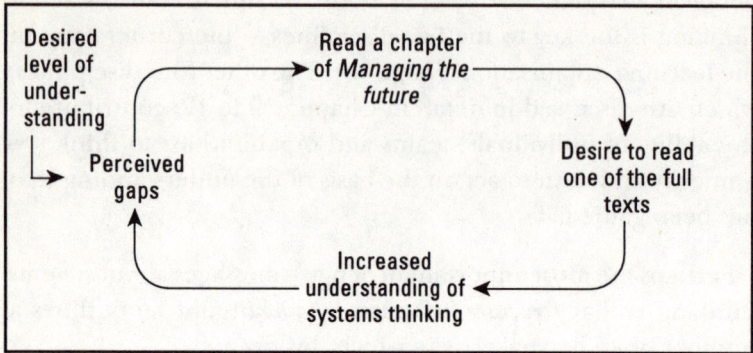

```
Desired
level of                    Read a chapter
under-                   →  of Managing the
standing                    future
    |        Perceived                      Desire to read
    └──→     gaps                           one of the full
                                            texts
                         Increased
                         understanding of  ←
                         systems thinking
```

This diagram can also be written as a story: I purchase and read *Managing the future*, which stimulates my desire to read the whole of Senge's book. As my understanding of systems thinking develops, the perceived gap (between my current understanding and my desired level of understanding) changes. As the gap changes I am inspired to read more of the texts that are discussed in *Managing the future*. And so on.

This way of seeing our actions demonstrates how structure influences behaviour. It enables us to see beyond single causes for each event that occurs. It also assists us to identify the feedback that we receive as the underlying structure unfolds.

Feedback within these circles of causality can either reinforce the pattern or serve to balance the trend. In addition, delays may occur which retard the impact of the actions being felt.

Senge complements his systems diagrams in Chapter 5 with diagrams of reinforcing circles (which demonstrate how small changes can snowball), balancing circles (to show the sources for stability and resistance to change) and diagrams which demonstrate the impact of a delay between taking an action and feeling the consequences.

An understanding of reinforcing processes, and of balancing processes and delays, are both essential to the adoption of a longer-term view. They can help people to:

- comprehend why certain patterns (the archetypal structures) occur again and again

- identify the fundamental causes of problems and not just the more obvious symptoms
- find the 'high leverage' responses: the 'actions and changes in structures (that) can lead to significant, enduring improvements' (page 114).

Senge's discussion of the five learning disciplines is supplemented by a consideration of several **key questions that learning organisations must face**. The answers advanced are based on the experiences of various prototype organisations which are trialling systems thinking and the four core learning disciplines.

The questions and answers discussed are:

- *How can organisations create an openness which moves them beyond the traditional focus on internal politics and game playing?*
  A two-fold response is required. First, the development of a shared vision to move individuals beyond just self-interest. Second, the disciplines of mental models and team learning can be used to promote an openness where people are encouraged to speak openly and honestly and also to challenge their own thinking.
- *How can an organisation establish the sort of localness which allows a decentralisation of responsibility whilst still ensuring that the organisation retains sufficient coordination and control?*
  Having responsibility for our own actions is a prerequisite for learning. Thus learning organisations devolve as much authority and power as possible to the local level. Coordination and control of localised organisations is exercised via corporate management's focus on development of shared vision (to guide local action) and improving the quality of thinking by using the mental models discipline. In addition, systems thinking can assist the local bodies to gain an appreciation of the whole and of the consequences of their localised actions.
- *How can managers go about creating the time for learning?*
  This comes down to redefining what is manager's work – so that the truly important roles of reflection and the examination of complex issues are not squeezed out by incessant and often unnecessary activity. Senge relates that, in Japan, when an executive is sitting quietly, there will be no interruption

because it is assumed that the executive is thinking. In America (and Australia, too) the assumption would be that the person has nothing important to do.

- *How can people balance the demands of work and family and ensure that personal mastery and learning are evident in both spheres?*
  A reading of the popular press reveals that this is one of the major questions of the 1990s. Senge suggests that part of the answer lies in an acceptance by the organisation of its responsibility to contribute to a better balance between work and family. This involves dispensing with the traditional view that the two are entirely separate domains. In fact, systems thinking encourages individuals to see the connection between their personal and professional lives. Of equal importance is the individual's need to clearly identify the balance that they desire (their vision).

- *How can we create the conditions whereby we can learn from experience in situations where we are unlikely to actually experience the consequences of our decisions and actions?*
  Simulations known as 'microworlds' facilitate learning through experience by compressing time and space to enable the consequences of decisions and actions to be felt. Microworlds are sophisticated simulations of reality that have been made possible by new computer technology. They assist managers to learn from experience, but with a degree of safety. Three specific microworlds are outlined in Chapter 17 of the book.

- *What work should leaders do in the new learning organisation?*
  Senge suggests that the leaders in learning organisations will play three major roles. They will be:
  - designers of organisations that can integrate and practice the five learning disciplines
  - stewards of the organisation's vision, articulating where the organisation has come from and where it is headed
  - teachers helping people develop a clearer appreciation of reality in the context of the big picture of underlying systemic structures and the purpose of the organisation.

Building a learning organisation is an ongoing process, not a single event. Thus Senge concludes by pointing out that the future is likely to see the development of new disciplines beyond anything contemplated today.

THE CHAPTERS

(The more significant ones are indicated by an asterisk)

Chapter 1	Summarises each of the five disciplines.
Chapter 2*	Illustrates the seven learning disabilities.
Chapter 3	Discusses a simulation exercise known as *The Beer Game* and the lessons that can be drawn from it.
Chapter 4*	Outlines the fundamentals of systems thinking.
Chapter 5*	Explains the tools of systems thinking.
Chapter 6*	Demonstrates how the management problems organisations face are often manifestations of a set of identifiable systems archetypes.
Chapter 7	Demonstrates the principles of leverage for bringing about improvement.
Chapter 8	Uses the example of People Express Airlines to illustrate the value of systems thinking.
Chapter 9	Outlines the discipline of personal mastery.
Chapter 10	Discusses the discipline of mental models.
Chapter 11	Explains the discipline of shared vision.
Chapter 12	Explores the discipline of team learning.
Chapter 13	Discusses openness as a counter to political game playing in organisations.
Chapter 14	Examines the importance of localness in encouraging genuine responsibility for actions taken.
Chapter 15	Investigates how managers create time for learning.
Chapter 16	Considers the issue of balancing family and work.
Chapter 17	Outlines the technology of the learning organisation known as 'microworlds'.
Chapter 18*	Discusses the roles and the work of leaders in the new learning organisation.
Appendix 1*	Outlines the basic practices, principles and essences of each of the learning disciplines.
Appendix 2	Outlines a number of systems archetypes and discusses their implications.

3
STEERING NOT ROWING IN THE PUBLIC SECTOR

David Osborne and Ted Gaebler – *Reinventing government: how the entrepreneurial spirit is transforming the public sector*
(Addison-Wesley, 1992, 405 pages)

ABOUT THE AUTHORS

David Osborne is a consultant to state and local governments. He is also the author of *Laboratories of democracy*. In 1993 US Vice-President Al Gore recruited Osborne as a consultant to the administration's National Performance Review, established to consider major changes in the Federal bureaucracy.

Ted Gaebler is the head of the Gaebler Group, which is a division of a California-based public sector management consulting firm, MRC. Gaebler has been the city manager of both Visalia in California and Vandalia in Ohio.

THE SIGNIFICANCE OF THIS BOOK

In part the importance of the book is related to the wide range of influential US figures who have endorsed its content. The most prominent of these is Bill Clinton who, while Governor of Arkansas and candidate for the Presidency, wrote:

> 'This book should be read by every elected official in America. Those of us who want to revitalise government in the 1990s are going to have to reinvent it. This book gives us the blueprint' (back cover).

The back cover blurb further says that '*Reinventing government* is not a partisan book. It focuses not on what government should do, but on how government should work. As such, its ideas have been embraced by both liberals and conservatives'. The book is heavily influenced by Deming's concepts of Total Quality Management, as is the case with Peter Senge's book, *The fifth discipline.* In particular, Osborne and Gaebler have started from the TQM premise that the customer is the most important person for the organisation and that, therefore, organisations must continually ask them what they want so they can direct their entire activity towards providing it.

THE AUTHORS' BASIC ARGUMENT

To some extent *Reinventing government* is a collection of success stories of how some Governments are meeting the challenges of our new information society.

They are stories about how these governments – mainly local rather than central – and especially the people who lead them, are behaving like successful business entrepreneurs.

This entrepreneurial approach involves: dispensing with arbitrary and restrictive rules and regulations; empowering employees at the local level; clearly identifying who the prime customers are and taking heed of what they have to say; and doing more with less.

The book is by no means anti-government. Rather it provides a pro-government perspective based on the view that industrial era governments, characterised by high degrees of centralisation and large, rule-driven bureaucracies, cannot meet the needs and challenges of the new information society.

New kinds of public institutions are therefore emerging which are more flexible and more customer-oriented. This trend mirrors what is occurring outside the public sector where organisations are promoting flatter management structures, decentralisation of authority and a greater focus on improving quality and customer service.

Government in the modern world will concern itself less with levels of resourcing, or of privatisation and ownership, and more with acting as entrepreneur so as to produce the most effect for the actions that are taken.

This does not mean, however, that governments will operate

exactly the same as businesses do. This is not possible, for a
number of reasons. For instance, our democratic system demands
that governments take their major decisions openly and this
affects both the processes used and the timelines adopted. What
the authors mean is that governments will take advantage of the
vast scope that exists for them to operate more like client-oriented
businesses do: seizing opportunities as they emerge; and continually striving to eliminate waste.

Osborne and Gaebler draw together the lessons of their collection of success stories into a set of **10 principles for transforming
the public sector**. These principles, which form the basis of a new,
entrepreneurial model of government, are:

STEER, RATHER THAN ROW

For generations the role of government has fundamentally been
to provide services which are paid for from taxes that have been
levied. As revenue sources have contracted, however, public
officials have increasingly been faced with equally unpopular
imperatives: raising taxes to pay for the services provided; and/or
eliminating some of the services.

In the short term the problem was made to go away by borrow-
ing money. But clearly that could not go on forever.

The alternative that is advanced by Osborne and Gaebler
involves a reconception of the fundamental role of government
to one of 'problem solving by catalysing action throughout the
community' (*Osborne and Gaebler*, page 28). This is what they call
steering, rather than rowing. In other words, government's role
becomes one of setting the direction, making policy, dispersing
resources and then evaluating the outcomes, rather than engaging in direct service delivery. A case of leading rather than doing.

Steering involves such things as establishing partnerships with
the business sector, mobilising and resourcing community sector
organisations and using market incentives to promote social
goals. In fact, the authors have identified 36 alternatives to
standard public sector service delivery which are detailed in
Appendix A of the book.

The advantages that are claimed for steering governments include: greater flexibility in responding to new and changed conditions; a greater likelihood that they will concentrate on the overall mission; and (because they can shop around for the best service) a greater willingness to experiment and to focus on comprehensive solutions to problems.

In the end, steering governments actually govern, rather than just administer.

EMPOWER COMMUNITIES TO SOLVE THEIR OWN PROBLEMS, RATHER THAN MERELY DELIVER SERVICES

This principle is built on the premise that people tend to be more committed to something they own than to something controlled by others. Empowered communities dealing with their own problems will, it is argued, generally outperform communities that are dependent on the provision of outside services.

The shift from full-time professionals to community provision is a response to two major factors: community demands for more power, manifested in the emergence of various action groups such as public transport users' associations; and the increasing trend for governments to contract out service provision to not-for-profit community organisations such as the State-based AIDS Councils.

Osborne and Gaebler (drawing on the work of John McKnight from Northwestern University) suggest that **the advantages that community empowerment has** over conventional professional service delivery include:

- a greater understanding of the community's real problems
- a tendency to tackle and solve problems rather than just deliver services
- the provision of *care* and not just *service*
- a greater degree of flexibility and creativity
- lower cost
- more effective enforcement of standards of behaviour (which is really an adjunct to *caring*)
- a tendency to focus on *capacities* rather than to respond to *deficiencies*.

Irrespective of the benefits, however, community ownership will not always emerge spontaneously. It is something that governments need to support and nurture by providing opportunities such as seed funding, professional advice and training for community members.

In addition, government cannot use community empowerment to absolve itself of the ultimate responsibility for ensuring that community needs are met. Since government retains the responsibility for steering, it must establish appropriate accountability mechanisms to ensure that resources and services are being delivered in a fair, equitable and efficient manner.

PROMOTE AND ENCOURAGE COMPETITION, RATHER THAN MONOPOLIES

The essence of this principle is summed up by John Moffitt, Chief Secretary to Massachusetts Governor William Weld, who said: 'The issue is not public versus private. It is competition versus monopoly' (page 76). This is because competition leads to a greater consciousness about costs and a better level of service delivery.

Osborne and Gaebler suggest that **the advantages of increased competition** are:

- greater efficiency and value for money
- pressure on monopolies to consider and respond to their customers' needs
- greater likelihood that innovation is valued and rewarded
- increased pride and morale of public sector employees (though the authors add the caveat that a degree of job security needs to be maintained for this to occur).

Competition in government can take many forms, including instances where:

- a public provider competes with private firms, as Telecom does
- private firms are invited to compete with each other to provide a public service, such as contracting out payroll management functions
- competition is encouraged between different public sector providers.

Osborne and Gaebler argue, however, that it is important that competition be carefully structured and managed, particularly if equity is a guiding principle of the steering government.

Governments, while promoting competition, also need to ensure that all segments of the market are adequately served and contractors are operating fairly and in accord with valued social goals such as equal opportunity.

BE DRIVEN BY MISSIONS RATHER THAN RULES

One of the early advantages of the bureaucratic system was that clearly specifying how things were to be done (through rules and regulations) helped to eliminate public sector nepotism and corruption. The other side of this coin, however, is that many modern public sector agencies have become so rule-driven that they are effectively paralysed in the face of new challenges and uncertainty.

Entrepreneurial governments focus on freeing up their employees to pursue their overall mission as flexibly and creatively as possible. This involves getting rid of the 'red tape' that ties up customers and service providers alike.

Central to **the creation of a mission-driven government** is:

- the elimination of unnecessary and outdated rules and regulations that have accumulated over time
- the replacement of line item budgets with more flexible budgets that allow for the movement of resources to priority areas and the retention of savings that have been made
- a transformation of the conventional 'civil service' personnel system into a more supportive system based on approaches such as broad-banded classifications, the payment of market salaries and performance-based pay.

With these sorts of changes in place, governments can set about defining their mission and then, around their mission, developing structures, operations and even a culture.

The original fear of rorting and abuse can be dealt with by instituting accountability measures that carefully monitor the outcomes of programs, rather than through myriad rules that simply use up resources to administer and observe.

BE RESULTS-ORIENTED BY FUNDING OUTCOMES RATHER THAN INPUTS

Governments have traditionally focused on inputs rather than outcomes. Entrepreneurial governments focus on outcomes because this promotes improved performance. In fact, one of the major lessons of the Total Quality Management (TQM) movement has been that organisations need to measure results in order to achieve them.

In recent years advances in information technology have led to the identification of more imaginative ways to measure performance than was previously thought possible. For example, curriculum profiles have been developed which enable school teachers and systems to assess how well students are learning and not merely how well they take a test.

Performance measurement is important because:
- there is a tendency for things that are measured to get done
- identification of the measures requires clarity about the purposes of taking the action in the first place
- it helps governments to focus on successful programs and reward success
- it makes governments learn from their successes and endeavour to correct their failures
- there is the potential to gain community support when governments can demonstrate that programs are succeeding.

Osborne and Gaebler do, however, point to the importance of identifying comprehensive and sophisticated performance measures. Thus Appendix B of their book is devoted to the art of performance measurement.

MEET THE NEEDS OF THE CUSTOMER RATHER THAN THOSE OF THE BUREAUCRACY

By contrast with the business sector, governments have tended to ignore their customers.

Since the funding of most public sector agencies comes directly from government, it is generally politicians and interest groups who are the focus of activity, rather than customers.

It is this factor, according to Osborne and Gaebler, that leads the public to perceive the government sector as an arrogant bureaucracy – a perception that can turn to frustration and anger when government red tape is compared to private sector efforts to please the customer.

This negative view of government is compounded by the tendency for the public sector to offer 'one-size-fits-all services' (page 168) rather than a range of customised products. This leads many consumers to opt for various private sector alternatives.

Entrepreneurial governments, however, have begun to listen to their customers and respond to their needs; and on pages 177-179 the authors outline 17 ways in which they can go about this.

A critical element of customer-driven government is a transformation of the bureaucracy and, in particular, the bureaucratic mindset. Many public sector systems are designed more for the people who run them than for those they are intended to serve. This is manifested in complex processes that ordinary citizens are unable to comprehend and find extremely difficult to penetrate. The archetypal story is of the person who is shunted from one department to another while getting no closer to resolving the problem that brought them there in the first place.

Entrepreneurial governments work on the development of user-friendly systems and processes which are easily accessed by their customers.

In addition, they often endeavour to establish one-stop shops that enable customers to meet all of their needs in one location rather than having to deal with a large number of different providers of services.

CONCENTRATE ON EARNING MONEY RATHER THAN JUST SPENDING IT

The culture of government involves spending money rather than earning it. As tax revolts have spread, entrepreneurial governments have been forced to consider ways in which they can:

- gain revenue from sources other than taxes
  and/or
- manage their expenditure more effectively while eliminating waste.

It is not, however, Osborne and Gaebler's intention to suggest that all public services should be operated purely for profit. Rather, they argue that there are a number of services that are subsidised by the taxpayer (such as the provision of certain recreational facilities) and that could reasonably become sources of profit for government.

The most common mechanism for raising money is the charging of fees for services provided, as already occurs in relation to various government utilities. Fees can be charged in full or be subsidised, either to ensure the provision of socially useful services, like public transport for instance, or for reasons of equity.

Osborne and Gaebler argue that an important benefit of a focus on earning as well as spending is that it leads to a concern for the investment side of outlays as well as the costs involved. This also encourages the adoption of a longer-term view towards outlays. A cost now can, over time, become a community investment.

It is not enough just to urge a more entrepreneurial approach to financial management. It is also necessary to provide **incentives** for public sector managers to be more goal-oriented. This could involve:

- instituting mission-driven budgets where managers can retain all or part of any savings or earnings that are made
- establishing specific (seed) funds for the promotion of innovative ideas
- identifying the true costs of services that are provided so that sensible decisions about pricing and subsidising can be made.

INVEST IN PREVENTING PROBLEMS RATHER THAN IN CURING CRISES

Osborne and Gaebler contend that one of the consequences of rowing rather than steering is a tendency to provide services which deal with symptoms rather than acting to prevent the problem from occurring. A good example of this is the way that environment-protection authorities often focus on pollution control after the event rather than ensuring an environmentally sound approach to start with.

By contrast, entrepreneurial governments not only focus on

prevention, but they also adopt a longer-term view in their planning and decision-making so as to anticipate the problems that could emerge. Osborne and Gaebler turn to the unlikely area of fire prevention to provide an example: the requirement for all new buildings to incorporate sprinkler systems.

While the electoral process tends to ensure that the focus of politicians does not extend beyond a few years, there are some instances that are cited of governments adopting a more far-sighted approach. The major processes that these governments have used include the establishment of futures commissions and the use of techniques of strategic planning based on a vision of where the organisation wants to be in five, 10 or even 20 years time.

Strategic planning has, in turn, been supported by a range of **political and financial measures**, such as:
- longer-term budgeting and the use of five- to 10-year revenue and expenditure projections
- the establishment of reserve or contingency funds to prepare for future needs
- the adoption of accrual accounting so that future expenditure obligations and depreciation are taken into account
- the promotion of more regional government to respond to the fact that many issues can no longer be handled entirely at a municipal level.

DECENTRALISE AUTHORITY RATHER THAN BUILD HIERARCHIES

As the knowledge and communication revolution spreads, and the workforce becomes more educated, a centralised system based on communication through a long chain of command becomes increasingly inappropriate. The need for quick and responsive government requires that workers at the local level be empowered to make as many decisions as possible.

Entrepreneurial governments have good **reasons for decentralising their decision-making**. They do it to become:
- more flexible and more able to respond quickly to local needs and circumstances

- more effective, because the workers at the local level are in the best position to develop solutions to problems that emerge
- more innovative, because new ideas are better able to emerge from the work of those who deal directly with customers
- more able to generate high morale, commitment and productivity, because the processes of participation and teamwork tap into the skills and enthusiasm of the workforce.

By decentralising decision-making, control through hierarchy is replaced by accountability through the articulation of a common mission and the continual measurement/evaluation of results.

Osborne and Gaebler suggest that participatory management is the cornerstone of decentralisation. It recognises that people become more committed and invest more of themselves when they have control over their work.

The **processes that generate participatory management** in government include:

- the creation of flatter hierarchies to avoid overcontrol
- the encouragement of team work
- a willingness to invest in the development of each employee.

SOLVE PROBLEMS BY INFLUENCING MARKET FORCES RATHER THAN BY CREATING PUBLIC PROGRAMS

Consistent with steering rather than rowing, entrepreneurial governments increasingly operate as brokers and facilitators rather than as direct service providers.

These governments endeavour to use leverage and intervention in the marketplace to produce desired outcomes. A good example is the way in which the Commonwealth Government has used tax incentives rather than government-initiated programs to promote research and development in industry.

Osborne and Gaebler regard this trend as representing a 'third way' (page 284), coming between state-controlled or state-administered programs and a completely laissez-faire, free-market approach.

There are many **ways in which governments can seek to structure and influence the market place**. The most common involve
tax credits and user-pays fees, but other mechanisms available
include:
- the establishment of rules such as, for example, town planning regulations, to govern the market place
- the creation or influencing of demand for particular goods
  and services as happens in the subsidising of child care
- the stimulation of private sector activity through a variety of
  means: the Victorian Government provided a good example
  of this when it granted a casino licence in exchange for a
  construction program in a tourist precinct (as well as the
  licence fee).

Despite their argument for more market-oriented government,
Osborne and Gaebler are quick to note the importance of balancing markets and community. Markets, they argue, are only one
half of the equation; especially if equity is a central concern. The
other half of the equation is community empowerment.

This twin focus on markets and community is what they call
'moving right and left at the same time' (page 305).

Osborne and Gaebler conclude their book by suggesting that
their 10 principles can serve as a checklist to 'unleash new ways of
thinking – and acting' (page 311). To illustrate this they briefly
apply the principles to the three major areas of health care,
education and the criminal justice system.

In essence, what is described in *Reinventing government* is a
fundamental shift in the whole way of thinking about the public
sector that amounts to a new paradigm of government; a paradigm shift that can be observed throughout the developed world.

THE CHAPTERS

(The more significant chapters are indicated by an asterisk)

Introduction*   Provides a thumbnail sketch of entrepreneurial gov-
                ernment in action and an explanation of why the new
                spirit is emerging.

Chapter 1*   Outlines the overall philosophy of an entrepreneurial
                approach to government.

Chapter 2   Discusses the empowerment of communities rather than of the bureaucracy.

Chapter 3   Explores the advantages of competition in the public sector and the ways it can be promoted.

Chapter 4   Argues for governments to be driven by their mission rather than by their rules.

Chapter 5   Focuses on the importance of outcomes and results rather than inputs.

Chapter 6   Examines the importance of a customer focus rather than a provider focus.

Chapter 7   Looks at enterprising governments which are concerned with earning as well as spending.

Chapter 8   Makes the case for governments seeking to anticipate problems in order to prevent them.

Chapter 9   Considers the promotion of participation and team work through the decentralisation of government.

Chapter 10   Looks at the potential for governments to promote change through the marketplace.

Chapter 11*   Brings together the 10 principles and briefly comments on the paradigm shift that is underway.

Appendix A   Outlines 36 alternative service-delivery options and some guidelines for choosing the best of them.

Appendix B*   Illustrates a number of important lessons in the art of performance measurement.

4
EMPLOYEE EMPOWERMENT AND NETWORKS ARE THE KEY

Tom Peters – *Liberation management: necessary
disorganisation for the nanosecond Nineties*
(Pan Books, 1992, 834 pages, extensive table of contents, preface)

⇒

ABOUT THE AUTHOR

Tom Peters is the author or co-author of three of the most successful management texts that have been produced: *In search of excellence* (with Robert H. Waterman, Jr.); *A passion for excellence* (with Nancy Austin); and *Thriving on chaos.*

Peters publishes a regular newsletter called *On achieving excellence* and has a PBS television show. He also writes a weekly column syndicated throughout the United States.

THE SIGNIFICANCE OF THIS BOOK

Undoubtedly part of the significance of the book derives from the importance of its author, a phenomenally successful management writer and presenter with several bestsellers to his name.

Liberation management is also important because it has been written as a sort of handbook for surviving and experiencing success not only in the 1990s, but also into the next century.

The book is based on extensive research from around the globe which focuses on real companies and real experiences. Hundreds of people were interviewed for it and thousands attended seminars throughout the world to provide Peters with feedback. Their experiences are included in the numerous chapters of the book and these are balanced by the inclusion of brief summaries of relevant research and journal articles.

To some extent *Liberation management* is an iconoclastic book

which challenges some of the 'truths' that Peters himself espoused in earlier years. In particular he questions the essence of
In search of excellence, that 'closeness to the customer' is the be-all
and end-all. He strongly suggests that corporate success might
depend just as much on the transformation of organisational
structure.

Peters' liberal use of metaphor, and the inclusion of extensive
quotes from practising CEOs, increases both the accessibility of
the book and the likelihood that key concepts will be remem-
bered.

THE AUTHOR'S BASIC ARGUMENT

Perhaps the central concept in the book, underpinning the whole
of Tom Peters' thinking, is the concept of **fashion**. Things are
moving so fast in the modern world that the only way to stand out
from the crowd is to start creating products to meet the needs of
customers that they don't even know they have yet.

That sort of approach to fashion demands liberated managers
who can exhibit 'flair and bravura ... (and pursue) breathtaking
failure as assiduously as success' (*Peters*, page xxx). Increasingly
they will work in brain-based organisations that involve global but
ephemeral networks and partnerships rather than fixed corporate structures.

With this as his underlying premise, Peters structures his book
around six major, and extensively illustrated, themes, and each
theme forms a section of the book.

Theme 1 – Necessary disorganisation: the new exemplars

Increasingly specialised food lines, varieties of beer containers
and customised building materials are all examples of the 'fashion' that Tom Peters has in mind.

Consumer items are no longer merely utilitarian. They are also
often fashion accessories – think no further than the mobile
phone.

Constantly changing fashions require us to redefine all of our
products and services, a requirement spurred on by the continual
emergence of new competitors and rapid advances in technology.

There is a constant search for the competitive edge. Peters calls this 'going soft' because of the inevitable connection to knowledge-based computer software as well as the focus on user friendliness and the '"entertainizing" of everything' (page 7).

Since fashion can be very fickle, Peters suggests that the organisations that survive (and thrive) will be those which are both fickle and, of necessity, decentralised. In effect, a network organisation which, in Peters' view, will operate according to certain **magic numbers**:

- One – to represent empowered individuals.
- Two to four – for the sort of micro-enterprises that increasingly provide a large range of the services sought by consumers.
- Seven to 10 – which is the number of people who generally compose a self-contained work group.
- Three to 12 – to cover the organisational project team.
- 12 to 20 – which applies to what Peters calls 'mini-enterprises': the sort of business units that deal with the entire process and product in a speedy and efficient way.
- 40 to 200 – which is the large number of people who might make up a constantly changing, but nevertheless ongoing network of individuals, units or businesses.

Peters suggests that the essence of the modern-day network can be captured in the metaphor of **the carnival** because:

- while the whole forms our image, it is the parts that we experience
- the essential unit is the booth, where provider and customer meet
- the 'underpark' or facilities are as important as the attractions for maintaining customer loyalty
- the market continually and speedily determines which activities endure and which fold
- there is a need to provide certainty and sameness while also ensuring that there are new surprises in store
- the carnival continually moves on and has no fixed address
- it has only a small core staff, but lots of networked/contracted activities

- the customer creates the experience from the range of opportunities offered
- it is an extremely dynamic concept and activity.

Peters advances three examples of corporations as carnivals:

- The firm **EDS (Electronic Data Systems)** because it is a knowledge-based corporation that focuses on providing solutions to meet the needs of enterprises. It is a project-based, non-hierarchical organisation, and it is struggling to be a genuine learning organisation.

  Above all, EDS is a collection of project teams, generally of eight to 12 staff who work together for between nine and 18 months, often alongside some full-time people from the customer organisation(s). Getting the job done, rather than maintaining clear, hierarchical reporting lines, is what matters most to them. According to Peters, EDS is 'loose, flexible and – due to the emphasis on accountability for results – disciplined' (page 26).

- **Cable News Network (CNN)** which is designed to provide news as and when customers want it: that is, 24 hours a day, rather than in fixed timeslots only a few times a day. At CNN decisions are made quickly by those closest to the action, and personal initiative is expected from all employees in order to cope with the demands of continually broadcasting live.

- **Asea Brown Boveri (ABB)** which has broken its eight major business sectors into a series of business areas. These in turn are sub-divided into a larger number of incorporated companies that ultimately consist of 5000 autonomous profit centres dealing directly with customers.

  Any central staffing is kept to minimal levels and focuses on promoting whole-organisation learning through continued information exchange.

Theme 2 – Learning to hustle

As David Vice, the Vice-Chairman of Northern Telecom, is quoted as saying: 'The nineties will be a decade in a hurry, a nanosecond culture. There'll be only two kinds of managers: the quick and the dead'. (page 59)

There is today a necessity to do everything faster, which is giving rise to what Peters calls the 'new hustlers' movement. But hustling in Peters' terms involves more than just speed. It also involves getting close to the customer and working in continually-changing networks to develop and market revolutionary, fashionable products.

Peters provides three case studies of firms that he believes are learning to hustle.

- **Titeflex**, a manufacturer of fluid and gas hoses that has virtually eliminated its former bureaucratic structures and processes and replaced them with customer-friendly, multi-disciplinary teams of employees empowered to make the decisions affecting their work.

  This development was underpinned by an openness which proclaimed that 'There are no limits to worker involvement' (page 69). Relationships also changed so that the remaining managers spent more and more time with employees on the shop floor, while workers met more regularly with customers.

- **Ingersoll-Rand**, where a highly successful new product was developed in a very short time by virtue of bringing together all the key players, assisting them to work as a team and letting them thrash out the issues themselves. Time and money were invested in working through shared concerns; important symbols such as the conduct of appropriate bonding activities were attended to; key suppliers were continually involved in the process; and, perhaps most important, end users were regularly visited so that the product could be designed around meeting their needs.

- The **Union Pacific Railroad**, which matched and surpassed its trucking competition (which had been leaving it for dead) by improving reliability through speedy and effective decision-making. They gained the confidence of their customers.

  Achieving this required the corporation first to recognise and admit the problem. They then had to eliminate the array of bureaucratic impediments to decision making and instead empower the direct service providers to solve customer problems.

As was the case with ABB (see above), the focus was on creating a matrix approach to organisation and management, but without establishing a new bureaucracy. This was achieved through the promotion of self-managing teams.

Theme 3 – Information technology: more, and less, than promised

Information systems are essential to the horizontal linkages that Peters discusses in the first two sections of *Liberation management*. They constitute the way in which people share data and communicate with each other.

Information technology is fundamentally changing the way we work and live. 'The world has been turned upside down, and the computer, along with telecommunication networks, is the engine of the revolution' (page 108).

Information has long been at the heart of a corporation's competitive edge, because it is information about the customers' specialised needs and wants that drives all activities in the marketplace. What is new is the growing recognition that this is the case. The growth in information networks through concepts and developments such as Bill Gates' 'information super highway' is also an important new trend.

Peters points out that information technology can take many **forms**:

- direct information-related products such as PCs and telecommunications
- computer-assisted design and the building of prototypes
- the use of computer simulations and modeling to invent new products as happens in genetic engineering
- what he calls the 'smartening of everything', whether it be our latest CD players or our new workplaces
- the use of computer-assisted manufacture to produce customised products in a short space of time
- the re-creation of old industries such as occurred with banking in the age of deregulation
- the development of new network companies through new connections

- the use of telecommuting to support self-employed entrepreneurs.

Information technology can also impact markedly on organisational structure. While some organisations were beginning to break down hierarchies prior to the 'age of information', the new technologies have greatly **speeded up** this development due to:

- the provision to 'outsiders' (suppliers, distributors, customers) of insider information and the 'informating' of employees
- the increased access to information from outside the organisation through electronic highways
- the ability to establish project teams which include participants from more than one physical location
- the tendency for the scale of operations to become progressively smaller (and more manageable) and for organisations to use networks to produce desired levels of 'bigness' when required
- the likelihood that organisations increasingly will become learning communities where knowledge is continually used to add value to all that is done.

Having illustrated the importance of information technology, however, Peters is quick to point out that it does not automatically lead to success. If new technology supports existing organisational dysfunctions it will only compound the problems being experienced. Thus it may be necessary to begin with the proverbial clean slate in order to simplify operations and (as taken up in depth in the next section) move beyond hierarchies to facilitate the sharing of information.

Theme 4 – Beyond hierarchy

This is by far the largest section of the book, reflecting perhaps the importance given to the breaking down of hierarchies.

Section 4 is also the site for Peters' *mea culpa* in relation to his past works. In particular he is at pains to point out that, while closeness to the customer is vitally important, it cannot be achieved without destroying any 'enormous, numbing, top-heavy organisational structure' (page 131) that may happen to exist.

For Peters this involves more than just flattening structures and eliminating layers of management. In fact he recommends a clean-slate approach whereby the whole organisation is redesigned from scratch.

For those who fear anarchy, he provides a detailed case study of **McKinsey & Co.** which, he argues, is one of the world's ultimate project organisations. At McKinsey all work is produced by small project teams which draw on expertise (from within and without) as needed, and work closely with the customer. Building networks is a key activity for employees and all are encouraged or expected to make connections with new partners.

A strong customer focus at McKinsey ensures that the firm does all it can to avoid becoming inflexible or bureaucratic. While the consultants certainly see themselves as part of McKinsey, their overriding concerns are to create and to manage their own work in the interests of their clients.

Peters' view of McKinsey is not all starry-eyed. He does point out that the support staff tend to have second-class citizen status and that 'squeaky wheels' are usually removed rather than oiled. Nonetheless, it is a very large and successful company with no strong evidence of hierarchy as we traditionally conceive it, and an ability to move with the times.

The unifying principle that Peters sees at McKinsey is: 'Create your own firm. It's up to you to take the initiative, start projects, seek out customers, build your own network' (page 146). It is this sort of fluid, project-based structure that enables McKinsey (or EDS or CNN, or many other companies cited) to shift course quickly as and when required.

Peters uses the McKinsey case study to introduce a new theory of organising. This theory underpins the entire fourth section of his book. It consists of 27 **organising propositions** encompassed here in the following 15 concepts:

- knowledge work is now the main work of organisations and the major source of value added
- most business will be done through seamless, horizontal networks where the middle-management role is no longer required

- work will predominantly be done by project teams which value and enhance individual expertise
- functional barriers in organisations will be eliminated and specialisation will be developed in the context of a concern for the whole product/process
- project teams that are established will focus on promoting interdependence between team members, trust and individual talent
- outsiders (such as customers and suppliers) will also belong to project teams whose life span will vary according to the nature of the task
- results will matter more than reporting lines and team members will spend more of their time out in the field
- increased customer contact will result in shorter feedback lines and peer evaluation will assume greater importance
- the organisation, while held together by its shared vision, will be subject to perpetual reorganisation
- learning/teaching/communication devices will be the basis of much of the value added and organisational learning will be highly rewarded
- applying information technology will be important, but the focus will be on providing all people with maximum access to all information
- project-management and network-management skills will be required by all employees
- the network's ability to undertake all tasks will be enhanced by its access to sub-contractors that provide a high-quality specialist function ('supersubs')
- commercial projects will increasingly be undertaken either by 'systems integrators' who establish and manage networks or by specialists such as supersubs or 'independent talents'
- power in the marketplace will be a product of the networks which comprise the organisation, rather than of the resources owned by the organisation.

Peters' term for firms which conform to this new theory of organising is: 'professional service firms'. Their *raison d'être* is to work on 'a discrete *project* for (and with) a customer; *thinking* their way through a unique opportunity to add value' (pages 159-60).

A good example of such a firm is the British 'events' company, **Imagination**, which operates with total flexibility, yet meets impossible deadlines, because the project team is all. This small project team approach is also more conducive to the customer contact that is so essential for success.

Professional service organisations can also be less permanent entities. Peters illustrates this by describing how his own PBS video lectures were produced by an ad-hoc team of specialists that came together only briefly for the task. While impermanent, the organisation had a clear task, a clear goal, a clear (albeit non-hierarchical) structure and its own culture derived from the knowledge that each member possessed of each other member.

Having outlined this example, Peters acknowledges that questions are often asked about the applicability of this project-team approach to more traditional manufacturing companies. To answer these questions he describes the experience of the Danish hearing-aid manufacturer, **Oticon**.

Since 1990, Oticon has sought to shift from a command structure to a problem-solving one. Jobs are designed to fit the people. Multi-skilling is encouraged and employees take responsibility for their own project team work. This new approach has been supported by a physical restructuring whereby barriers to communication (walls) have been removed and the movement of offices encouraged.

From the experiences of the firms he has cited, Peters identifies a number of **musts** for organisations if they are to operate as professional service firms:

- understand that a project team is not a committee: the accountability for results, the commitment of those involved and the focus on the customer make it much more than that
- understand the importance of project management. On pages 212-14 he outlines some fundamental principles for being an effective project manager
- get your accounting right (this can require an overhaul of the old, functionally-delineated costing methods)
- start now

- reconsider the concept of 'career': your working life must be dominated by projects.

These 'musts' give rise to a set of basic **organisational building blocks** which specify that:

- every employee must be a business person: an empowered individual in possession of all of the information required to meet the needs of the customer
- the self-contained, self-managing work team, working on its own projects, is the basic unit of the organisation
- the success of these teams depends on 'the missing x-factor: trust' (page 249)
- the right size for an organisation is becoming progressively smaller (Peters actually suggests that the magic number for a market-scale unit is between 50 and 60), and 'bigness' is achieved through networking.

So is there a need for a corporate centre? Peters is inclined to answer Yes on the basis that **a corporate centre can still provide**:

- a sense of vision (or, as he puts it, a 'point of view')
- a network for organisational learning
- a few selected central services
- a degree of market power and attractiveness to investors.

Corporate centre aside, it is clear that more and more companies are eschewing vertical integration in order to establish more manageable units that concentrate on what they do best. They then form strong network alliances/partnerships for everything else.

These networks, which are increasingly global in scope, give new meaning to the concept of size in relation to any individual corporation. 'New big', which can be very big indeed, is 'network big' (page 305). Many of Japan's largest corporations are really just networks that rely on large numbers of small contractors.

The practice of networking subcontractors can be applied equally to services provided by the firm's own head office. Central service providers within an organisation can be required to compete with outsiders for contracts, and the users of central services can be expected to foot the bills from their own budgets. In some cases (as occurs with BHP's service companies) such central units can even seek to win contracts with customers outside the host firm.

Whichever course is followed, the effect is to make central services as subject to the marketplace as any of the contractors with which they (now) compete.

Irrespective of the size or location of the network, however, conscious management of it is required. Above all, there must be investment in relationships: with employees, with contractors and with customers.

And management must accept the ambiguities of the modern market and the ambiguous nature (the 'necessary disorganisation' of the book's title) of the network organisation. Indeed, Peters suggests that the term 'organisation' should always be in inverted commas.

This style of management is often performed better by women than by men. Peters quotes research by Sally Helgeson suggesting that **women managers** are more likely to:

- see interruptions as opportunities to work on strengthening relationships
- focus on the long term
- see any negotiations in the context of the ongoing relationship
- be inclusive of all team members.

Having examined management styles for network organisations, Peters returns to one of the book's predominant themes: that knowledge is the major source of value added. This means that knowledge management becomes central to an effective network organisation. This, according to Peters, involves more than just the use of information technology.

The **knowledge management structure** (a term he uses in preference to 'learning organisation' because he sees it as more specific) is based on:

- the sharing of knowledge (McKinsey has established the position of Director of Knowledge Management)
- a philosophy which promotes collective learning
- promoting the sharing of knowledge by encouraging people to discuss ideas and seek feedback on them

- building recognition for learning into individual performance evaluations
- using databases and publications to share information and
  ideas.

This knowledge management structure can be supported by
appropriate 'space management' (page 413) to encourage rather
than inhibit communication and the sharing of information. For
instance, any physical plant or office that happens to exist can be
arranged around multi-functioned teams rather than separate
departmental areas; and employees can be allowed to locate
themselves where they can best carry out their tasks.

This spatial approach can then be complemented by using the
available technology (e-mail, for example) to network people and
create the sort of collaboration that utilises the total brain power
of the organisation.

The effect of all of this is to encourage the horizontal learning
that is necessary in a world where 'customer perceptions are
"horizontal"' (page 449). At a hotel, for instance, customers experience a horizontal slice of the organisation's functions (valet
parking, check-in, room service, etc) rather than a vertically
structured department.

Peters suggests that 'horizontal rather than vertical' is the single
most important idea in his book. It is a concept which encourages
people to address issues and think in terms of the whole rather
than their own particular specialisation.

Peters concludes this long section, 'Beyond hierarchy', by
pointing to some **paradoxes of the new organisational approach**
that he has described:

- as firms increasingly become organised into tight networks,
  they also increasingly become collections of extremely independent (and hence disorganised) units
- as the firm becomes smaller the network to which it belongs
  becomes bigger
- accountability for work undertaken is balanced by commitment to and support for network partners
- individual autonomy is balanced by stronger partnerships
  with others

- as individuals develop their own expertise, functional (specialist) barriers are eliminated.

Theme 5 – Markets and innovation: the case for disorganisation

It is clear from *Liberation management* that Tom Peters is an unashamed supporter of the market as the best means to promote innovation and better service in an increasingly 'fashionised' world.

Today's market is, in his view, moving so fast that constant innovation is the only viable response. 'Try anything! – then try something else' (page 483). Continual experimentation is vital because success, while often a matter of chance, is generally built on a series of failures; and because experimentation can counteract the tendency for successful firms to become complacent and stale.

Peters argues that, to remain innovative and marketable, today's firms need to:

- disorganise: they should continually re-invent themselves and try new things to meet the market's ever-changing demands
- promote strong competition both internally and with other firms.

Understanding these things is, he suggests, a prerequisite for effective leadership in the modern world.

The **German Mittelstand** (small and medium-sized companies) have these understandings down to a fine art in Peters' view. They begin by clearly identifying their market niche: the core activity that they will pursue through thick and thin. They then apply the latest technology to the production of a quality product which enables them to compete vigorously in the marketplace.

Consistent with the messages from the previous section, 'Beyond hierarchy', their smallness enables them to eliminate unnecessary production and decision-making delays. Smallness also facilitates the development of closer relationships amongst employees (including employer-union relationships) and stronger identification with the customers.

Peters brings together his thoughts on the market and the views outlined in 'Beyond hierarchy' to develop a set of **imperatives for marketising** that encompass:

- rethinking scale: essentially a reiteration of the 'unit small network big' concept
- a preparedness to, in the words of the Nike advertisement, 'Just do it!': to try things and see how they work
- a passion for one's product combined with a willingness to allow questioning and to encourage irreverent thinkers to pursue their ideas and make waves
- a style of management that unleashes the creativity and imagination of the workforce. Since the human imagination is a thing that tends to defy management, Peters calls this process 'loosening up', a term which embraces both the need to welcome and accept the views of others, and a willingness to pinch good ideas from anywhere at all.

Theme 6 – Fashion

Peters' theme of constantly-changing fashion underpins the greater part of *Liberation management*. It is appropriate, therefore, that Peters ends his book with a discussion of fashion itself. Fashion dominates because, when all the organisational restructuring has occurred, the company still has to have a product and a standard of service that are unique in some particular way.

The number of new products being released each year is growing almost exponentially. The release of new brands of familiar items accounts for some of it, and the rest is made up of totally new products designed to meet newly identified needs.

The sheer degree of product specialisation that is occurring constitutes 'a clear break with the past' (page 652). The consequence is that there is a race on not only to surpass one's competitors, but also to supersede one's own product before it is superseded by others. And a major element of this race is the continual 'softening' of products as information technology makes them smarter, and as entertainment is used both as a marketing device and as a product in its own right.

The fashionised market is forcing organisations to focus

continually on what makes their product special. This is illustrated by significant research quoted by Peters which shows that brand name and the accountants' concept of goodwill now constitute the major sources of value in company takeovers. This all means that building the brand is an increasingly important activity for all corporations.

This is especially the case when the apparent shrinking of our globe, mainly through telecommunications, is accompanied by an increasing diversity of human behaviour and tastes. Global corporations therefore need to be keenly aware of regional and cultural differences so they can cater for these. Once these differences are understood, the company can set about providing the kinds of goods and services that make their customers 'glow and tingle' (page 677), and want to say 'Wow!'.

This '**wow factor**' derives from the product itself, from intangibles such as reliability and excitement, and even from a first-class instruction manual. Firms that get both the product and the intangibles right will not only retain customers, but they will also attract some they have never had and regain customers they have previously lost.

In order to achieve the wow outcome Peters suggests that firms will need to:

- work together ('intertwine') with customers, not just listen to them
- move beyond mere customer satisfaction and seek to gain customer commitment
- converse with customers about the product and, if necessary, train them in its uses
- provide unconditional guarantees about the quality (and value) of the product
- try to conceive of big issues in terms of personal experiences
- attend to the service process and continually seek to improve it
- view customers as being in a life-long relationship with the firm and not merely performing a one-off transaction
- remember that treatment of the customer matters as much as product quality and price

- build data bases of customers and potential customers to enable dealings with them to be personalised
- above all, take the time to tend to the *relationships* in their business.

All of this requires firms to reorganise their processes so that they are designed purely and simply to serve the customer rather than the 'convenience of the "production function"' (page 740). Peters calls this 'customerising' (rather than 'customising') because it is dependent on the active involvement of customers in the defining of needs and the joint development of products and processes to meet those needs.

Peters sums up his book by suggesting that the two-fold answer to the fashion demands of the 1990s and beyond is, in fact, embodied in the title of his book:

- the **liberation** of all employees to take whatever actions or initiatives they believe are necessary to serve their customers
- **disorganisation** into autonomous units in order to enable that liberation to occur.

THE CHAPTERS

(The more significant chapters are indicated by an asterisk)

	leading product by creating cross-functional teams that really worked together.
Chapter 7	Discusses how the Union Pacific Railroad slashed middle management, empowered its frontline employees and took on its trucking competitors.
Chapter 8*	Considers the implications of the fact that the manipulation of information will, increasingly, be the source of profit and value added.
Chapter 9*	Explores how information technology impacts on organisational structures and, in particular, contributes to the breaking down of hierarchies.
Chapter 10*	Focuses on McKinseys as a case study of an 'unglued' organisation and outlines 27 propositions for a new theory of organising.
Chapter 11	Introduces the concept of 'professional service firms' as illustrated by the UK-based company Imagination and by David Kelley Design and Chiat/Day/Mojo.
Chapter 12	Continues the examination of professional service firms by describing how Peters' own PBS video programs were put together by ad hoc project teams of talented specialists.
Chapter 13	The projects and professional service firms concept is extended to the Danish company Oticon; the world's leading manufacturer of hearing aids.
Chapter 14	Completes the discussion of projects and professional service firms by exploring some ground rules for 'projects for all'.
Chapter 15	Introduces a discussion of the basic organisational building blocks by arguing that every person must be a business person.
Chapter 16	Outlines the second of the basic organisational building blocks: promotion of self-contained work teams.
Chapter 17	Points to the importance of trust, illustrated (ironically) by the example of a US prison.
Chapter 18	Completes the discussion of basic organisational building blocks with a focus on 'market scale units' of 50 to 60 people.

Chapter 19   Outlines the experiences of Germany's producer of
              restaurant ovens, Rational, and explains how it has
              benefited from the type of smallness that Peters
              describes in his book.

Chapter 20*   Introduces a more detailed discussion of networks,
              particularly as an alternative to vertical integration.

Chapter 21   Continues the discussion of networks with a consid-
              eration of the sub-contractors that Peters calls
              'supersubs'.

Chapter 22   Considers the issue of 'marketising' the firm by
              making head-office services compete for business in
              the same way that network subcontractors do.

Chapter 23   Shows how collaboration through networking can
              enable firms to concentrate on the things that make
              them most competitive; but also warns against the
              risk of going stale if a monopoly results.

Chapter 24   Describes life in a network and the challenges of
              managing one.

Chapter 25   Explores a range of further metaphors, drawn from
              quantum physics, aboriginal folklore and elsewhere,
              to describe the network model of an organisation.

Chapter 26   Discusses how organisations accumulate and share
              knowledge, once again with major reference to
              McKinseys, and points to the importance of taking
              knowledge management seriously.

Chapter 27   Continues the discussion of knowledge manage-
              ment structures by examining the importance of the
              physical location: 'space management' to produce
              'cultural change'.

Chapter 28   Shows how knowledge management structures use
              information technology to share knowledge and
              pool the organisation's brain power.

Chapter 29   Completes the discussion of knowledge manage-
              ment structures with a consideration of ways in which
              real (as opposed to nominal) expertise can be de-
              veloped and tapped in an organisation without a
              hierarchy.

Chapter 30   Examines the sociology of becoming more horizontal, and broader in vision, by thinking in wholes.

Chapter 31   Returns to the theme of trust and reiterates its importance for organisational effectiveness.

Chapter 32*   Sums up the large section called 'Beyond hierarchy' and points to some paradoxes of the new organisational paradigm.

Chapter 33*   Examines the messy and unpredictable nature of the market and the way in which the market encourages innovation and risk taking.

Chapter 34   Further explores the disorder of the marketplace and the importance of 'market injection' strategies such as selling off new units or promoting competition through appropriate licensing of new technology.

Chapter 35   Explains how Germany's small and medium-sized companies have operated to great effect in the marketplace.

Chapter 36   Introduces a series of chapters on 'marketising' imperatives with a discussion of the need to rethink scale in relation to modern organisations.

Chapter 37   Outlines the second marketising imperative: a bias for action, or 'just do it!'.

Chapter 38   Explains that the third marketising imperative is a passion for one's product and a willingness to question whether it is being produced in the best possible way.

Chapter 39   Describes the final marketising imperative: to 'loosen up' management so as to liberate employee creativity.

Chapter 40   Demonstrates that change is extremely complex and that, since the difference between success and failure is often merely a matter of luck, marketisation and radical decentralisation may well be the only viable responses to change.

Chapter 41*   Discusses how fashion is leading to the continual transformation of virtually every product.

5
A PERSPECTIVE ON NETWORKING MANAGEMENT

David Limerick and Bert Cunnington – *Managing the new organisation: a blueprint for networks and strategic alliances*
(Business and Professional Publishing, 1993, 270 pages)

➡️

ABOUT THE AUTHORS

David Limerick is Professor of Organisational Behaviour, Planning Head of the Graduate School of Management and Dean of the Faculty of Commerce and Administration at Griffith University in Queensland. He is widely published in international journals and has consulted to a wide range of private and public organisations.

Bert Cunnington is a Senior Lecturer and the Deputy Dean of Commerce and Administration at Griffith University.

THE SIGNIFICANCE OF THIS BOOK

This management text has been something of a best seller. It provides a full description of the organisation for the 21st century.

The authors have effectively captured the importance of building networks and strategic alliances in a climate of dramatic change. They also explain the skills that will be needed by managers who wish to lead their organisations to success in this climate.

The book has been very well received by the human resources profession, as evidenced by the success of David Limerick's 1993 national seminar tour for the Australian Human Resources Institute (AHRI).

The Bulletin magazine described *Managing the new organisation* as 'an excellent book' in which 'the problems, challenges and opportunities, in an era of unprecedented discontinuity, are very clearly outlined'.

HR Monthly considers it to be a 'thoughtful and important book, indispensable to the new-age HRM manager who wants to remain at the cutting edge of management thought'.

THE AUTHORS' BASIC ARGUMENT

Limerick and Cunnington, like many others, view the 1980s as a period of profound, rapid, discontinuous change: a period when conventional wisdoms were overturned.

Organisations, they say, were particularly affected. By the end of the decade, organisations had become network organisations characterised by collaborations, partnerships and alliances.

Such structures have quite different management require-ments, of course, and the issues they raise are 'beginning to plague managers of the new organisation' (*Limerick and Cunning-ton*, page 8).

The authors suggest that there are, broadly, three models for thinking about these changes and the issues they generate. Each model shows us that the last part of the twentieth century is an era of individual autonomy and organisational decentralisation.

The three strands of thinking are:
* post-modernism
* neo-humanism
* disorganised capitalism.

Although there are significant differences between them, each acknowledges that managers are now confronted with autono-mous individuals, people who possess enhanced access to infor-mation and knowledge, in their organisations.

The new organisational form that has emerged from the dis-continuities of the 1980s is, in Limerick and Cunnington's view, the network organisation. This structure is characterised by col-laboration between autonomous individuals, and between groups, in pursuit of a shared goal. The essential management task is, therefore, to facilitate collaboration and broker the strategic partnerships which underpin the new organisation.

This, they suggest, requires a fundamental shift in the managerial mindset or 'blueprint'.

To assist us in understanding this blueprint, which the writers call the 'fourth blueprint', Limerick and Cunnington first outline the characteristics of three other blueprints that have dominated western management over the years.

THE FIRST BLUEPRINT: THE 'TRADITIONAL CLASSICAL' APPROACH TO MANAGEMENT

Growing out of the Industrial Revolution, this functional, almost machine-like, approach to management lasted at least until the late 1930s. It was characterised by high degrees of job specialisation (the Taylorist division of labour), close supervision of work and workers, and a strict hierarchy of authority and control.

The role of managers in this situation was to plan, coordinate, motivate and control; and the workers they supervised were fundamentally disempowered.

Although there were significant attacks upon it, this dehumanised structure did work for a long time, delivering mass production to meet the demands of the emerging market.

It started to come undone in the Great Depression when, arguably, it failed to deliver.

THE SECOND BLUEPRINT: THE HUMAN APPROACH TO MANAGEMENT

The well-known Hawthorne studies resulted in a shift in focus from the formal, hierarchical structure to the more informal work grouping. Greater attention was paid to how people felt about their job and their co-workers. Managers became more concerned with the social needs of groups and individuals. The interpersonal skills of managers consequently assumed greater importance. Managers started to do more than just supervise.

This trend was strengthened by the impact of the Depression. A fundamental questioning began. Managers started to focus more on linking the individual, the group and the organisation. Organisations started to become flatter in structure.

In the boom years, the years of contentment, the second

blueprint enjoyed considerable success. It was not until well into the 1970s that the third blueprint simply overwhelmed it.

THE THIRD BLUEPRINT: SYSTEMS APPROACH TO MANAGEMENT

The challenges to the second blueprint emerged when the US monopoly over world markets was challenged by stronger foreign competition and when the Americans started to concern themselves with self-fulfilment as well as with economic success.

The coming together of these two trends stimulated the development of a new paradigm of management which focused on the outside as well as the inside of the organisation.

The open systems approach to management, or systems model, emerged in the 1970s as an alternative to the two earlier blueprints, in part because it eschewed single, universally-applicable approaches to managing organisations. It was a contingency approach whereby managers were encouraged to analyse the environment in which they operated and then select the appropriate organisational form for that environment.

This approach acknowledged that the impact of an environment is never uniform across an organisation. So, managers began to focus on sub-systems, or teams, as key units. Team building became an important activity; and often the unity of the team was promoted at the expense of individual differences. Interdependence, openness and group cohesion became paramount.

In the late 1980s, however, the fundamental assumptions of the systems approach began to be challenged, and their effectiveness in an age of discontinuous change was questioned.

THE FOURTH BLUEPRINT: THE COLLABORATIVE ORGANISATION APPROACH

Unlike organisations which had followed the systems approach, companies operating at the end of the 1980s were, according to Limerick and Cunnington, increasingly characterised by:
- decentralisation to autonomous and often unrelated business units
- attempts to choose and/or influence the environment in

which the organisation operated
- a willingness to acknowledge the differences within the organisation and its sub-systems
- a growing interest in the seemingly non-rational aspects of an organisation: its culture, for instance, and the management of meaning
- the emergence of active and empowered individuals.

These factors have resulted in the emergence of a new blueprint for management which is appropriate to our times. The new blueprint is based on:
- dealing with on-going, discontinuous change
- organising around small, loosely-coupled units
- networking as required within and outside the organisation in order to achieve synergy
- promoting 'collaborative individualism'
- uniting the organisation through its shared vision and mission
- exercising 'transformational leadership' to hold it all together.

Above all else, the fourth blueprint is about loosely-coupled systems: small, autonomous units collaborating with each other, and with external units, by networking.

Several factors have led to the emergence of these network organisations, but the predominant one has been the phenomenon of **discontinuous change**. 'An organisation', suggest Limerick and Cunnington, 'is facing discontinuous change when its past does not prepare it for the future' (page 50). And this aptly describes today's world where technology and communication have created a global marketplace in which money and information know no borders.

The fourth blueprint emerged, in Limerick and Cunnington's view, because an entrepreneurial rather than a competitive culture is required to deal with discontinuous change. Organisations characterised by networking and the formation of strategic alliances are more likely to be entrepreneurial because they focus on what they do best and contract out other activities to whoever can provide them most efficiently.

The authors argue that there are, in fact, two basic types of strategic network:

The internal network

In an internal network, units in an organisation operate autonomously but collaborate with other units to produce commonly-desired outcomes. It's really a case of what Tom Peters refers to as 'new big' being 'network big'.

The external network

This is, in Limerick and Cunnington's view, 'the dominant organisational form of the 1990s' (page 66). The phenomenon of discontinuous change makes it impossible for any organisation to do all that it wants to do internally. The best people to meet the needs of organisations will often be outside them; so **strategic alliances** are formed with these outsiders. Such alliances appear to take one of three basic forms:

- the regional cluster: an alliance between small organisations on a regional basis. Perhaps the best known example is the group of firms in Italy's Emilia-Romagna region whose collaboration has contributed significantly to economic growth in that country
- the industry cluster: a number of small firms that share a specialisation and a geographic area. Silicon Valley is a particularly good example, focused, as it is, on the computer industry
- the global alliance: whereby, when the global marketplace has virtually eliminated national markets and national corporations, firms forge alliances on a world scale.

Many of these alliances are temporary in nature, coming together to perform a particular task and then disbanding when the task is done.

The fundamental advantage of networking as an approach is that it enables an organisation to concentrate on what it does best, whilst contracting out other activities to its allies. But there are other advantages too: networking fosters innovation, because research and development resources can be pooled; networking can maintain a focus while still customising products as necessary; and lastly, networking can strengthen access to the opportunities that exist in the global marketplace.

Networking is not, however, without its **problems**. Many alliances and networks have failed because of such factors as:

- an inadequately defined purpose and a lack of clarity about the network's boundaries
- the desire for unit sovereignty at the expense of the network
- asymmetry between network partners
- excessive concentration on the short- rather than the long-term goal
- difficulties inherent in managing across different cultures.

Thus, the establishment of a successful network is dependent upon new approaches to management and a whole new set of management skills. Limerick and Cunnington suggest that there are, in fact, nine '**essential elements of effective network management**' (page 89):

Liberate your managers
It is the managers of the units who are ultimately responsible for the activity of networking. So local managers become empowered and the hierarchy becomes flatter.

Develop your boundary roles
Managers should look outwards; accept responsibility for managing their unit's relationships with other groups and individuals.

Develop your communication systems
Networks need to pay particular attention to horizontal communication; and since they tend to be geographically dispersed they should get support from management for high technology communication systems.

Get the mindset right
Managers need to believe that collaboration is the best way to operate in today's global marketplace. Lip service is unlikely to bring success. There is, of course, no magic formula for instilling a new mindset; but activities such as training have an important contribution to make.

Each of the remaining five elements is directed at strengthening the degree of **trust** within the network:

Set up the alliance carefully
There is a need to take time to choose alliance partners carefully in order to ensure compatibility and a real potential for synergy.

Define the focus
The objectives of the alliance must be clearly defined so the nature and scope of the arrangement are clear to all partners involved.

Manage the soft issues
Since trust is the essential component of any strategic alliance, it needs to be continually reinforced and managed. This involves: ensuring equity in the relationship between partners; focusing on the long-term relationship; and showing leadership in the creation and building of the organisational vision.

Manage the hard processes too
The other side of trust is obligation. Managers need to negotiate their contract of participation in the network carefully so that they can meet the commitments they undertake.

Manage the network control systems
Communications technology should be used to facilitate the management of organisational relationships by ensuring the free flow of information required by both internal and external networks.

Management competencies such as these nine essential elements have assumed great importance for Limerick and Cunnington because we now live in a paradox: individuals have been empowered; yet, at the same time, they must work together to achieve desired outcomes. 'It is the age of *collaborative individualism*' (page 114).

Individual autonomy is at the heart of Limerick and Cunnington's concept of collaborative individualism because individuals are the source of new ideas and the energy to see them through. Nonetheless, they do need to work together, to collaborate in networks, in order to achieve the common mission.

What binds people together, then, is the commitment to a shared mission rather than any sense of group belonging *per se*. This is a 'post-teamwork, not an anti-teamwork phenomenon' (page 116). It is a collaboration that avoids the dangers of group think (the 'corporate citizenship' of the third blueprint). Within it people are encouraged to think creatively and take risks (the 'collaborative individualism' of the fourth blueprint).

In the third blueprint the corporate citizens were seen in terms of their organisational role. Each individual gave service, loyalty and commitment to the organisation in exchange for security and an on-going career.

For individuals in loosely-coupled networks, however, people's roles are constantly changing. The structures within which they work are temporary arrangements to facilitate collaboration. Their commitment is to the task rather than to the organisation; and the concept of a long term-career no longer has meaning.

Thus, **managers (and workers) in the fourth blueprint** are:

- autonomous: they make their own judgments and decisions
- proactive: they initiate their own collaborative activity and take action to achieve the network's mission
- empathic: they take responsibility for the management of meaning that holds the network together
- intuitive and creative: they are prepared to ask questions and think laterally
- transformational: they take on leadership and, where necessary, seek to create the new vision which inspires others to commit themselves
- politically skilled: they see the big picture and manage the politics that inevitably emerge within the network and between the network and its environment
- alliance-oriented: they can make the connections within the loosely coupled organisation
- mature: they know who they are and possess a clear set of

values to guide their involvement in the network.

Managers possessing these skills and capacities can extend the role of management to encompass 'vision and identity management' (page 161).

Limerick and Cunnington call this sort of management 'metastrategic management'. Their **metastrategic management cycle** consists of four elements that bring together 'vision, identity, configuration and organisational action' (page 168):

- founding vision: a clear picture of the type of business which the managers at least are seeking to create
- identity: a shared understanding of the values and the mission that will drive the organisation. Identity is what provides continuity of direction for actions taken in an environment of discontinuous change
- configuration design: an operational model for pursuing the vision in conformity with the organisation's identity. This model needs to bring together the organisation's strategy, structure and culture
- systems of action: the practical activities that are undertaken in order to meet specific customer needs: in effect, the organisation's processes, including its routines and its rituals.

In a formal sense, then, Limerick and Cunnington view metastrategic management as moving from vision to identity, from identity to a configuration design, and then from there to systems of action. Not surprisingly, the authors also point out that there are precious few examples of ideal behaviour; and in many cases the organisation's actions take over to the point that the founding vision and identity get lost.

Given this, Limerick and Cunnington suggest that the key strategic process for network management is the development of a shared vision of the network, together with the identification of its values and its mission. Once that is achieved, it can be translated into the more operational elements of strategy, structure and culture which enable management to link together the various systems of action of the network partners.

The **enactment of the management cycle** tends, in Limerick and Cunnington's view, to go through three basic phases:

- founding (phase 1): where the actual founder(s) of the net-work initiate the whole cycle, from vision through to action, to deliver the product. This phase is really a period of discontinuity
- consolidation (phase 2): the time when the organisation is succeeding in what it has set out to achieve and the network is operating in the marketplace.
- renewal (phase 3): a new period of discontinuity. This phase commences once the organisation realises that the environ-ment has changed in such a way as to call into question the original (and previously successful) metastrategic design. There is, for example, a fundamental change in consumer tastes requiring radical revision rather than incremental change.

   The development of a new vision in turn requires a whole new metastrategic design.

From phase 3 the cycle proceeds to consolidation and renewal as new discontinuities develop; and so on.

In all three phases, the organisation's leaders have a critical role in formulating the network's vision and identity. This 'manage-ment of meaning' is one of the most important tasks of fourth blueprint managers, because it is the vision and the identity of the network that provide it with its cohesion through each of the phases of the metastrategic management cycle.

Since these three phases really involve a continual shift between states of continuity and discontinuity, the management of mean-ing requires an approach where the organisation's vision and identity are constantly reappraised. 'This means establishing a *learning organisation* that has a self-transcendent capacity' (page 202).

Based on the research they have conducted with organisations, Limerick and Cunnington suggest that a CEO's four major **tech-niques for managing meaning** within networks are:

- language and slogans: the use of images with which networks identify themselves
- legends and models: the identification of organisational heroes who embody the organisation's values

- systems and sanctions: the use of organisational processes, together with rewards and sanctions, to reinforce values and behaviours
- self modelling: the all-important use of personal example.

In effective networks the use of these techniques does not stop at the CEO. It extends to other empowered individuals who make up the network and share responsibility for continually questioning the vision and identity of the organisation.

This questioning is important because discontinuous change can occasion the need for the organisation to alter its overall vision substantially, and hence its metastrategic design. The authors call this sort of change 'transformational change' because it can transform the organisation's entire identity. Often it falls to transformational leaders to define a new vision and sell it to the network.

For Limerick and Cunnington, there are five **critical activities** that contribute to this transformational style of leadership. They encompass efforts to:

- rekindle vision
- change structure and culture
- change mindsets
- change power structures
- empower others.

By focusing on consolidation and transformation, these managers begin to operate in the new paradigm of **action learning**. This involves an approach to management that encourages:

- (organisational) self-reflection so as to 'transcend and critique' (page 220) the current vision and identity
- actual initiation and control of the network by the partners and line managers.

To be effective, however, this approach needs to be embodied in specific management activities. Thus Limerick and Cunnington proceed to outline a 'coherent **set of managerial actions**' (page 231) to deal with networks characterised by the twin forces of autonomy and collaboration. These actions are:

- structural: where managers focus on building relationships and communicating across the network. The structure, they

argue, needs to be flattened so that line managers are empowered to make their own decisions. Technology should be
used to support the sharing of information and ideas.

- individual: where people are assisted to see themselves as
  autonomous individuals operating within the network, rather
  than as network resources. Individuals need to be supported
  in developing the mindsets and skills required to operate
  effectively in the fourth blueprint organisation. They can
  then focus on the assets they bring to a strategic alliance and
  continually develop those assets.
- organisational: where managers focus on metastrategy and
  the management of meaning. New processes and relationships need to be developed to operate in the fourth blueprint
  paradigm, and as far as possible the network should function
  as an action learning community.
- inter-organisational: where networking skills, especially the
  skills and processes of partner selection and boundary management, are improved, if necessary by drawing on external
  expertise.

Limerick and Cunnington conclude their book with a discussion of empowerment in network organisations and its relationship to the broader social issue of systemic discrimination. In
particular they suggest that fourth blueprint managers increasingly will seek to tackle discrimination not only because social
justice is a worthwhile community aim in its own right, but also
because the network organisation is most effective when it can use
all of the resources available to it.

Thus, a key task of the fourth blueprint manager is the **management of diversity**. This involves:

- action inside the organisation: the development of clear
  values and policies to guide action, supported by empowerment programs and the use of sanctions where necessary

and

- action outside of the organisation: engaging in a debate on
  how social structures and processes (such as the legal system
  or communication systems) can be used to promote and
  protect diversity.

Limerick and Cunnington's point is that 'the very act of devolution creates problems of power balancing both within and around fourth blueprint organisations' (page 247). The necessity to deal with these problems will generate not only a central problem for managers, but also, perhaps, a new, fifth-blueprint organisation.

THE CHAPTERS

(The more significant chapters are indicated by an asterisk)

Chapter 1   Traces the changes that occurred during the 1980s that resulted in the new network approach to organisation and a whole new approach to management.

Chapter 2*   Introduces the notion of blueprint to study the management of organisations and argues that the three blueprints of the past are being replaced by a fourth management blueprint based on collaboration and alliances.

Chapter 3   Examines the growing trend towards networking within and between organisations and the consequent formation of strategic alliances.

Chapter 4*   Considers various experiences of managing networks and outlines nine principles for successful network management.

Chapter 5   Discusses the trend away from corporate citizenship and toward collaboration between autonomous individuals.

Chapter 6   Outlines the concept of 'metastrategic management' and examines a management cycle consisting of vision, identity, configuration design and systems of action.

Chapter 7   Explores the issue of the learning organisation or 'action learning community' and the task of managing meaning within that organisation.

Chapter 8   Discusses the issues, the opportunities and the challenges that face the fourth blueprint organisation, with a particular focus on the management of diversity.

6
A CEO's APPROACH TO IMPROVING CUSTOMER SERVICE

Jan Carlzon – *Moments of truth: new strategies
for today's customer-driven economy*
(Harper & Row, 1989, 137 pages)

ABOUT THE AUTHOR

Jan Carlzon is a former President and Chief Executive Officer of Scandinavian Airlines (SAS). His achievement in turning around the fortunes of SAS has guaranteed him a reputation as a dynamic and remarkable business leader. Carlzon's success at SAS followed on from similar experiences at Vingresor, Sweden's largest tour operator, and Linjeflyg, Sweden's major domestic airline.

THE SIGNIFICANCE OF THIS BOOK

The book has been a best seller throughout the world and has been translated into 16 languages. A great deal of this success has been founded on the fact that *Moments of truth* was written by a practising CEO. In fact, John Naisbitt, the author of *Megatrends: ten new directions for transforming our lives*, describes it as 'the best book on leadership by a CEO' (front cover).

The appeal of the book lies in the fact that it is highly anecdotal and practical, drawing on Carlzon's substantial business experience.

Carlzon has set out to explain how he transformed three major corporations in the modern customer-driven world. In particular he has provided advice to other business leaders on: the development of strategy; organisation structure with a customer focus; motivation of employees; and communication within the organisation.

The book, as Tom Peters says in his foreword, is 'chock-a-block full of instructive stories and practical advice' (*Carlzon*, page ix). He concludes his foreword by suggesting that it 'provides examples, suggestions and, above all, a new philosophy – from someone who has been on the firing line and achieved brilliant turnaround successes in record time' (page xiii).

THE AUTHOR'S BASIC ARGUMENT

The 'moment of truth' which gives the book its title is the first brief encounter between customer and front line employee. It is a moment that determines how the customer is likely to view the whole organisation.

Tom Peters, in the foreword, illustrates this moment in terms of how an airline might deal with a situation where a sharp edge on a loose panel tears the stockings of a passenger who has just sat down. Are the employees empowered to deal with it on the spot or do they have to go through a long, hierarchical chain to gain a response?

The key to a successful organisation is, according to Carlzon, total orientation to serving the customer: becoming a customer-driven organisation. The goal is the satisfied customer because loyal customers are the best asset any organisation can have in this modern world: a world where quality and service are the sources of competitive advantage.

Carlzon goes on to suggest that the customer's image of the organisation derives not so much from its material (capital) stock, but from experiences with its people. It is the continual contact between employees and customers that will determine the success or otherwise of the organisation. 'They are the moments when we must prove to our customers that SAS is their best alternative' (page 3).

Good customer contact rests on empowerment of employees to meet the customer's needs. If the organisation is rule-driven and employees have to process requests through a lengthy chain of command, then the moment of truth will have passed.

Thus Carlzon argues that the traditional hierarchy must be turned on its head. A customer-driven organisation must be decentralised, with front-line employees empowered to make the day-to-day decisions that affect their continued interaction with the customer. As those layers of management which merely relay information and decisions up and down the hierarchy are progressively eliminated, the organisation will develop a flatter structure.

The **role of senior management** in the customer-driven organisation becomes one of true leadership:

- setting the direction
- communicating the vision throughout the organisation
- creating the environment in which employees can most effectively operate
- ensuring that employees are adequately trained to respond to the customer's needs.

To illustrate his philosophy Carlzon discusses his transformation of his own style of management at Vingresor and Linjeflyg. He tells of how he commenced his presidency at Vingresor, at the tender age of 32, by issuing instructions and seeking to fulfil the authoritarian 'boss' role that he believed he had been given. As a consequence, a lot of decisions were made on the basis of relatively little information, knowledge or even experience.

It was only the intervention of another senior manager, who queried Carlzon's leadership style, that led him to realise that his role was not to make all the decisions, but to create the 'right atmosphere' (page 8) for others to work more effectively.

When he started his reign at Linjeflyg four years later, his first act was to assemble the entire staff in an aircraft hangar and address them from atop a ladder on the state of the company. He also explained that the only chance of turning it around was if the staff themselves accepted responsibility for the task.

The consequence was development of a comprehensive strategy aimed at transforming Linjeflyg from a production-driven to a customer-driven organisation. This plan included an organisational restructure that turned the traditional organisation upside down.

Carlzon points out that a critical element of the turnaround was a decision to reduce fares substantially for off-peak flights, coupled with a marketing approach that tapped the psychology of the people who might use these flights. But equally important, in his view, was the decision to take staff into his confidence and to involve them. It generated a high degree of excitement and enthusiasm for the challenge that confronted the company. As a consequence, it was the staff themselves who identified many of the organisation's most successful ideas.

When Carlzon became CEO of SAS he built on these earlier experiences and applied the principles of customer orientation to the most basic and universal of corporate activities: cost cutting.

Prior to his arrival, the approach to expenditure reduction had been characterised by taking a slice off all bits of the organisation. This applied even to those functions that customers wanted and for which they were prepared to pay.

Carlzon's approach was to focus on service improvement to increase market share and generate revenue. This involved the development of a new business strategy with the clear goal of profitability: establishment of a specific niche for SAS. The niche chosen was to be known as 'the best airline in the world for the frequent business traveler' (page 23).

The consequence of this strategy was that they ceased to view expenditure as a problem to be reined in, but as a resource for enhancing their competitiveness. Thus, expenses became a means of achieving the goals of the organisation; and all spending was examined with this end in mind. If expenditure did not serve a goal then it could be phased out. When it did serve a goal, consideration was given to whether or not the organisation was spending *enough* to ensure that SAS increased its competitiveness. Cost-cutting was, therefore, balanced by additional investment.

This cultural shift in the organisation's approach to expenditure added further strength to Carlzon's continual efforts to promote employee involvement. All of the organisation, from CEO to front-line employee, was working to improve customer service, and it was taken as read that they collectively held the key to improving market share.

Given this overall organisational context, Carlzon's view of his own role is very much one of being the **leader** of SAS. Not leadership in the sense of knowing all of the fine detail of the organisation's operations, or of making all the decisions related to this. Rather, leadership in terms of:

- assembling the knowledge and skills needed to make the decisions that have to be made
- creating the environment in which the organisation operates
- establishing the systems to support the delegation of responsibility for the organisation's operations.

Leadership, in Carlzon's view, involves building 'an organisation that can work to achieve the goal and establish measures that guarantee you are moving in the right direction' (page 34). The qualities that are required for the job are, therefore, not specific technical or product knowledge. Instead, they are general qualities such as:

- good business sense
- an understanding of how the different parts of the organisation, the people and groups within it, interrelate
- an ability to think strategically, beyond the mere detail to the big picture
- the capacity to understand and manage change
- an ability to articulate the vision and goals and then communicate these throughout the organisation.

The leader must identify a business strategy for the organisation which is designed to meet the customer's needs. The leader then organises in a way that best enables the organisation to pursue that strategy.

To achieve this it is often necessary to begin by clearly specifying, from the customer's perspective, what business you are actually engaged in. This approach can affect the way in which the organisation's employees deal with the customer. For example, if the automobile companies see themselves as providing the service of land transport, rather than just making cars, then they will probably focus more on the overall product they provide to the customer than on the technologies associated with automobile production.

It's a case of starting with the customer and the market rather than with the technology and the product. 'Then the means of production is tailored to give the customers the best possible products' (page 49).

When members of senior management learn to become leaders, the front-line employees, says Carlzon, will be empowered to make all operational decisions. This flattening of the pyramid is essential if employees are to serve the needs of the customer. It also critically impacts on the resultant image that the customer has of the organisation.

In effect, 'everyone is now a manager of his (*sic*) own situation' (pages 60-61), empowered to respond to the moment of truth as an employee may deem appropriate at the time.

Carlzon does, however, sound one note of caution here. It is easy, he suggests, to lose middle management who may feel that they have been demoted, or left with no role. It is necessary, therefore, to ensure that middle managers are trained and encouraged to take on their new role of supporting the work of the front-line staff, rather than just supervising others and implementing rules.

This **new middle-management role** is, in fact, essential in a decentralised organisation. It is this group of managers who are responsible for:
- motivating the front-line staff
- translating the organisation's goals and strategies into practical and achievable local objectives
- assembling and providing the resources that are needed by staff to achieve their objectives.

So, flattening the pyramid results in a more effective and productive organisation that serves its customer better and taps into the hidden energy of its employees.

Flatter structures can also encourage the sort of risk taking – the courage to act – that enables an organisation to move continually forward. The decisions at Linjeflyg and SAS were by no means revolutionary; but Carlzon and his colleagues acted on them in the context of an overall business strategy where previously they had been ignored.

This sort of risk taking is not, in Carlzon's view, the exclusive preserve of senior management. It needs to percolate throughout the whole organisation. There needs to be a cast of mind within the organisation that says 'it is all right to make mistakes'. People need the security of knowing that, when they take a risk, they will be supported by management; that their errors (as opposed to negligence or incompetence) will be things to learn from and not something for which they are punished.

To get to this point, however, all employees must first be persuaded to share the vision of the organisation. They then need to be convinced that they can and should accept responsibility for implementing the vision.

Clearly, effective **communication** is critical to these conceptual changes; so much so that, as Carlzon sees it, communication, with employees and with the customer, should occupy more of the leader's time than any other activity.

Communication with others is, not surprisingly, more than merely what is said; it is also what is done. By example, Carlzon describes the experience of abolishing the executive dining room at Linjeflyg. Managers started eating in the staff canteen, inevitably reinforcing the verbal messages that we're all in this together and that it's the results we achieve that really count. 'Setting a good example is truly the most effective means of communication – and setting a poor one is disastrous' (page 95).

Almost as important as communication, in Carlzon's view, is the **measurement of results** that are achieved. This is particularly so when the organisation is concerned to ensure that the needs of the customer are being met.

Measuring results assumes added importance in a decentralised organisation because it provides:

- a major source of feedback on local actions: (are they contributing to the achievement of both corporate *and* local goals?)
- assistance in the identification of otherwise unnoticed service problems: (does anything need fixing?)
- praise where praise is due: (is anyone's contribution going unnoticed?) Self-esteem is a very important commodity in a service organisation.

Employees should be rewarded for valuable contributions made,

says Carlzon. It should not be forgotten, however, that two of the
best rewards available are real responsibility and real trust. They
reward; and they also greatly increase efficiency and effectiveness.

By 1984 SAS had accomplished its goal: it had attained the status
of 'Airline of the Year'. There was now a new problem, however,
because the company had not determined what it wanted to
achieve *after* that. So, in the absence of a clear new direction, the
sense of unity in the organisation started to break down. People
began to establish competing personal goals because there was no
overall shared vision to pursue.

The company had to find a new challenge. Carlzon chose to
reassert the fundamental commitment to improved customer
service as this challenge; and, as a direct result, a potentially disastrous situation was turned around. Employees rallied enthusias-
tically. In fact, the reaction was so overwhelmingly favourable that
Carlzon was inspired to seek a longer-term challenge for SAS.
This turned out to be preparing for deregulation.

Inevitably the launching of this long-term goal led to the
development of new strategies based on an analysis of trends
overseas. SAS was now once again well on the path to what Covey
and others have called the process of self renewal.

THE CHAPTERS
(The more significant chapters are indicated by an asterisk)

Chapter 1*	Outlines the concept of the 'moment of truth' and its implications for the creation of a customer-driven organisation.
Chapter 2*	Describes how Carlzon went about transforming Vingresor and Linjeflyg by liberating the energy of their employees.
Chapter 3*	Describes Carlzon's experience at SAS where customer service became the guiding force for expenditure and cost cutting.
Chapter 4	Explores the elements of leadership in an organisation.
Chapter 5	Shows how to use customer analysis to determine an organisation's strategy.

Chapter 6   Discusses the breaking down of hierarchies through
                a flattening of the pyramid.
Chapter 7   Looks at the importance of encouraging and sup-
                porting risk taking within the organisation.
Chapter 8   Considers the communication of the organisation's
                vision and the need to convince employees of their
                responsibility for carrying it out.
Chapter 9   Discusses the importance of imparting vision and
                strategy to unions and to boards of directors alike:
                getting them both on side.
Chapter 10   Examines the importance of measuring results to
                ensure customer satisfaction.
Chapter 11   Argues that a sense of self worth in employees leads
                directly to confidence, creativity and effectiveness.
Chapter 12   Considers the need for on-going improvement within
                the organisation.

7
BECOMING A MORE
EFFECTIVE PERSON

Stephen Covey – *The seven habits of highly effective
people: restoring the character ethic*
(The Business Library, 1990, 340 pages)

ABOUT THE AUTHOR

Stephen Covey is the chairman of the Covey Leadership Center
and the non-profit Institute for Principle Centred Leadership. He
is the author of six books, and in 1993 he won the prestigious
McFeely Award, presented by the International Management
Council, for his significant contribution to management education.

THE SIGNIFICANCE OF THIS BOOK

The back cover of the book quotes ringing endorsements from
some of the gurus of modern management, notably Tom Peters
(*In search of excellence*), Ken Blanchard (*The one minute manager*)
and Rosabeth Moss Kanter (*When giants learn to dance*). In addition, these cover notes are complemented by seven pages of praise
from 31 prominent people ranging from Steve Young, quarterback
for the San Francisco 49ers; to Ariel Bybee, mezzo-soprano at the
Metropolitan Opera; and James C. Fletcher, Director of NASA.

Covey's books have been phenomenally successful, selling more
than five million copies worldwide. His speaking engagements
are sold out wherever they are conducted; as evidenced by his May
1994 flying visit to Australia.

Covey's work is extremely influential in the corporate sector.
The Covey Leadership Center engages in leadership development throughout the world, and it has more than 100 of the

Fortune 500 companies as its clients. When General Motors in the United States was creating its newest division, the Saturn Corporation, for instance, the company turned to Stephen Covey for assistance and extensively used his training video on the seven habits of highly effective people. AT&T has designed its leadership training seminars around the principles that are embodied in Covey's book.

There is little doubt that the significance of the book is in part linked to the inclusion of application suggestions for each of the seven habits which readily lend themselves to training and development activities.

THE AUTHOR'S BASIC ARGUMENT

Covey's whole approach is premised on the view that the way in which we perceive the world, our personal paradigm, has a profound impact on how we behave. In addition, the ways we perceive ourselves and others have a habit of turning into self-fulfilling prophecies: the Pygmalion effect. Thus, in relating to others and in dealing with the various situations we face, we need to be conscious of the perceptions that colour our views.

This leads Covey to conclude that an individual's personal effectiveness is more a product of character than of particular techniques employed: 'what we *are* communicates far more eloquently than anything we *say* or *do*' (*Covey*, page 22).

We can genuinely examine and question our paradigms when we know what they are; and we can also become more open to the views and perceptions of others. And sometimes then we can experience a paradigm shift, an altered world view. This often happens with events such as the onset of parenthood where we undergo a substantial shift in our thinking and our priorities.

Covey's seven habits of highly effective people form a paradigm of thinking that derives from a set of character-related principles, including integrity, humility and fidelity. 'It's a principle-centred, character-based, "inside-out" approach to personal and interpersonal effectiveness' (page 42). It starts with the self and promotes both increased independence and effective interdependence.

When Covey uses the term 'habit' he is referring to the unconscious things we do, as a matter of course: the things that determine how effective we are. Thus, they are not easily changed: it takes work.

Each of the seven habits amounts to a combination of **three dimensions**, and for success we need to work on each of them:

- knowledge: what to do and why
- skill: how to do it
- desire.

The seven habits are an integrated package for enhancing personal and interpersonal effectiveness. By working on each of the seven habits we can, he argues, progress through a **maturity continuum**: from

- dependence: where we are reliant on others

  to

- independence: where we accept responsibility and do things for ourselves

  and then to

- interdependence: where we collaborate to produce outcomes beyond what we can achieve on our own.

The first three of the seven habits, which Covey calls the 'private victories', are concerned with the self-mastery that is necessary to move from dependence to independence. These three habits are the foundation stone for the 'public victories' (habits 4, 5 and 6) that are necessary for interdependence. Renewal, the seventh habit, encircles all of the others and is concerned with continuous development and improvement.

THE PRIVATE VICTORIES
HABIT 1 – BE PROACTIVE

This habit is concerned with the principles of personal vision.

It is because humans are capable of self awareness that they can analyse their experiences, learn from their mistakes and alter their habits.

Many people adopt a reactive approach to the world, responding to particular stimulus. However, 'between stimulus and response is our greatest power: the freedom to choose' (page 70).

Proactivity is about exercising the freedom to choose. Being proactive involves taking responsibility for one's own life, taking control and making choices about how one responds to events, rather than being a victim of circumstances.

By seizing the initiative we can seek to shape what happens and thereby determine the circumstances that affect our lives: in other words, working on those things that we can do something about. A good example of seizing the initiative is when we undertake further study or training, not only to develop new and deeper understandings, but also to improve our chances of gaining particular employment in the future.

Proactivity underpins the other six habits discussed by Covey as each of them places the responsibility for action directly on the individual. They all start from the question, 'What can I/we do?'

Choice of words is important to proactivity because words can create realities. A particularly good example is the way that people use the phrases 'I have to' as opposed to 'I choose to'. The former term is an abrogation of personal responsibility for one's actions whereas the language of 'choice' assumes an ability to control one's own life.

While Covey advocates a more proactive approach to life, he does point out that there is another side to this coin. We can choose the actions we take, but we cannot choose the *consequences* of those actions. Sometimes we may choose a course of action that leads to consequences that we would have preferred did not occur. The proactive response to this is to treat these choices as mistakes to be acknowledged and learnt from. In this way we can build success from the experience of failure.

HABIT 2 – BEGIN WITH THE END IN MIND

This habit focuses on the principles of personal leadership.

It is a habit which invites us to identify goals in our lives so that they can serve as the guiding framework for all that we do. Each of our actions can then be considered in the context of what really matters to us.

Covey likens this habit of beginning with the end in mind to the blueprint that a carpenter uses when building a house: it is carefully drawn up before any construction even commences and then referred to regularly to ensure that the task is in accordance with the plan. The blueprint is the mental or first creation which precedes the physical or second creation.

A proactive person naturally identifies the end in mind. This is because such a person takes control rather than allowing other people or events to determine what happens.

And a proactive person is a personal leader, because leadership is about transcending the daily management of our lives in order to identify our direction and the goals we seek to achieve.

This quality of personal leadership is, according to Covey, built on our human capacities for imagination and conscience. Imagination allows us to envision the end we have in mind, whilst conscience determines the framework or guidelines within which we can seek to develop our full potential.

These two qualities, together with the quality of self awareness referred to in habit 1, 'empower us to write our own script' (page 103).

We can do this by developing a **personal mission statement** which addresses:

- character: the type of people we want to be
- contributions and achievements: what we want to do and achieve
- values and principles: the bases of what we do and how we behave.

Covey then proceeds to provide a set of steps for developing this personal mission statement in conformity with the core paradigms – the centre – of our lives. In particular Covey suggests that we should endeavour to centre our lives on a set of correct principles derived from deep and abiding human truths that can provide us with our own security, wisdom, guidance and power.

The steps are:

- identify the centre that currently governs our lives: are our lives centred on family? friends? work?
- shift our paradigm to ensure that we operate in a balanced, principled way, meeting the full range of requirements for operating as a proactive person with a clear end in mind.

This is no easy task. To help in tackling it Covey suggests that we consider structuring our personal mission statements in terms of the various roles that we play: spouse, parent, worker, etc.; and then develop appropriate goals for each of these roles.

By being clear about the range of roles we fulfil, we can keep all of them in mind to ensure a balanced and principled approach.

HABIT 3 – PUT FIRST THINGS FIRST

This habit deals with the principles of personal management.

It is a habit that really grows out of the first two habits because day-to-day activity flows from a proactive approach to life and this approach leads, as we have seen, to the end we have in mind. The first-things-first habit is concerned with effective self-management in accordance with the life we have chosen to lead. We exercise our independent will to make the daily decisions and choices that put first things first.

The first two habits enable us to determine which things do come first. The third habit is about ensuring that those things are actually dealt with first.

Needless to say, the skills of time management are very important for habit 3 as they help us to prioritise, to ensure that the important things get done, that they are not deferred just because we may not like doing them.

Covey discusses time management at length. He provides a model for consideration in the form of a **time management matrix** which is in fact concerned less with time management *per se* than with managing ourselves. It is a model that particularly focuses on being proactive enough to direct ourselves to the really important activities that await our attention, rather than becoming consumed by the urgent, but often unimportant, matters to which we feel compelled to react.

When we are effective people we focus on reducing the amount of unimportant activities we deal with, irrespective of their apparent urgency. We can then work on the things that really matter such as long-term planning and the development of stronger personal relationships. This inevitably involves prioritising what we do, resisting the various pressures we may feel and then, when necessary, being prepared to say 'No'.

The irony is that by adopting this longer-range approach, the volume of day-to-day crises is likely to reduce because we are working on preventing the *causes* of problems and crises.

Covey suggests a **tool for self management** (pages 162-8) which, on a weekly basis, involves the four key activities of:

- identifying the various roles we perform
- selecting our goals for the week
- scheduling our activities to achieve our goals
- adapting on a daily basis.

The difficulty lies not so much in developing the approach as in remaining true to it and actually 'living it' (page 169).

Critical to living it is the act of delegation: giving other appropriately-trained people the responsibility for various functions so that we can concentrate on what both Covey and Peter Senge call 'high leverage' activities. Real delegation, where people are empowered to adopt their own methods to achieve the desired results, is at the heart of effective personal (and professional) management.

THE PUBLIC VICTORIES

'Effective interdependence can only be built on a foundation of true independence' (page 185).

Prior to discussing the three public victories, the bases of effective interaction with others, Covey introduces the metaphor of the **'emotional bank account'** (page 188) to refer to the degree of trust that's been built up in the area of relationships. Through our actions we can either make deposits in this account or make withdrawals. And, if we are not careful, we can become overdrawn. The main deposits we can make take the form of:

- making a real effort to understand the other person
- attending to the little courtesies and kindnesses that matter to others
- keeping commitments and promises
- being clear about what we expect of another person
- acting with integrity
- acknowledging any withdrawal from the bank, such as breaking a promise, and making a sincere apology for it.

HABIT 4 – THINK WIN/WIN

This habit comes from the principles of personal leadership. Effective interpersonal leadership is, indeed, based on the habit of thinking win/win.

Win/win is not only a technique, it is also a philosophy which promotes continual and conscious effort to seek mutually beneficial outcomes from our interactions with others.

'Win/win is a belief in the Third Alternative. It's not your way or my way; it's a *better* way' (page 207).

It derives from viewing each situation as a cooperative endeavour rather than treating it as a competitive exercise.

The alternative approaches to thinking win/win are:

- win/lose: often involves the exercise of power to bring about an outcome whereby one person wins because the other loses
- lose/win: the reverse situation whereby a person chooses to lose in order to be a martyr, or in order to appease someone else
- lose/lose: the outcome of two win/lose personalities meeting, often manifested in a mutual desire to get even at a later date
- win: where a person focuses solely on winning and is oblivious to the implications for anyone else.

Each of these approaches may be appropriate depending upon the circumstances. For example, most sports competitions are clearly designed to result in winners and losers. Alternatively, there may be occasions where it is appropriate to lose because another person really needs a win.

In the longer-term, however, it is win/win thinking that is most likely to contribute to lasting, productive relationships. Win/win is the only option if we are seeking true interdependence.

This is not to suggest that it is always possible to identify a win/win outcome. There may be occasions where there is no solution that is mutually acceptable to all involved. In these circumstances Covey suggests that the appropriate response is 'No deal'. In other words, in the absence of a win/win outcome, we just agree to disagree. This is preferable to forcing through a resolution that fails to satisfy one or more of the parties.

Win/win thinking is, according to Covey, based on five interrelated aspects of human life:

- character: being people of integrity, maturity and a sense that there is plenty available to satisfy everyone. (Note that these are the qualities developed by habits 1, 2 and 3).

- relationships: enabling us to go out and create win/win relationships founded on trust and mutual respect (See references above to the concept of the emotional bank account).

- agreements: giving substance and direction to win/win thinking. We should clearly specify aspects of any agreement such as what is to be done, when, what parameters apply to doing it, what resources are available, what standards are to be achieved, how and when the project is to be assessed, and what consequences flow from the assessment.

- systems and processes: supporting our win/win thinking. For instance, there is little point in seeking to encourage collaboration between departments if the organisation requires people to compete against each other for limited rewards.

HABIT 5 – SEEK FIRST TO UNDERSTAND, THEN TO BE UNDERSTOOD

This habit is founded on the principles of empathic communication.

Covey suggests that often our desire to resolve a problem is so great that we act without first diagnosing what is actually wrong. To have effective interpersonal communication, however, it is necessary to begin by understanding (making a diagnosis) before seeking to be understood (prescribing).

This involves a fundamental paradigm shift because most people listen in order to respond rather than to understand. We view other people's experiences through our own paradigms.

Very few people practice what Covey calls the highest level of listening: empathic listening, where we seek to understand the other person emotionally as well as intellectually.

Empathic communication involves more than just the techniques of active listening. It also involves a genuine attempt to understand the other person at a deep, human level. This requires us to move beyond the **usual ways in which we listen** to others:

- evaluatively: to determine whether we agree with the other person or not
- probingly: asking questions from our own perspective on the situation
- so as to advise: based on our own life experiences
- interpretively: trying to work the other person out in terms of our own understanding and behaviours.

By contrast, the **skills of empathic listening** involve:

- using active listening techniques, such as repeating the content of what has been said to indicate that you are attending
- rephrasing the content to indicate that you are thinking about what has been said
- reflecting feeling so that you focus on how the other person feels about what they are saying
- (a combination of the previous two skills of rephrasing content and reflecting feeling) trying to really understand what is being said.

These skills will, however, only be effective if they are accompanied by a genuine desire to understand the other person. In the absence of such a desire the use of the skills alone is likely to be perceived as an attempt at manipulating the other person.

Clearly empathic listening can take a great deal of time. But it constitutes a major investment in the emotional bank account which can bring substantial rewards in our long-term relationship with another person.

Great understanding, and an appreciation of the different perceptions that people hold, is essential to achieving the sort of win/win outcomes that were discussed in habit 4.

Having sought to understand, it is then necessary to be understood. This involves effectively presenting our views in such a way that the other person can understand and in a way which demonstrates an appreciation of their concerns and objectives.

Seeking to understand, and then to be understood, opens the

way to the more effective interpersonal relationships that are necessary for true collaborative action and synergy.

HABIT 6 – SYNERGISE

This habit is based on the principles of creative cooperation.

Covey views synergy as the culmination of the first five habits Simply put, synergy is that state that is sometimes achieved by humans where the whole is greater than the sum of the parts.

'The essence of synergy is to value differences – to respect them, to build on strengths, to compensate for weaknesses' (page 263).

The experience of synergy is similar to Senge's descriptions of team learning. It is based on the belief that people collectively are *able* to produce greater learning and better outcomes than they can produce alone.

Synergy requires a high level of communication coming, in turn, from a high degree of trust and cooperation.

Low level communication tends, rather, to produce defensiveness and generally results in win/lose or even lose/lose situations.

A medium level of communication is more respectful, but is still not based on the sort of empathic understanding considered in habit 5.

High levels of communication that make synergy possible can often result in new and creative outcomes way beyond what any of the participants originally thought possible. In addition, the creative process which leads to these outcomes can be a pleasant and enjoyable experience for those involved.

Pursuing synergy involves us in transcending the either/or paradigm that most of us adopt and instead collectively seeking the third alternative. This third alternative is not merely a compromise half way between two opposing viewpoints. It is a solution that is better than either option because all people involved can feel good about it. It is a solution that derives from communication and dialogue, from a process that accepts that different perceptions are to be valued: not 'I'm right, you're wrong', but 'We may both be right because we perceive the situation differently'.

HABIT 7 – SHARPEN THE SAW

This habit is built on the principles of **balanced self renewal.**

It is concerned with promoting a balanced approach to renewing each of the major aspects of our lives. Thus it focuses on:

- physical renewal: exercise, diet and the management of stress
- spiritual renewal: the continual clarification of values and commitments to others
- mental renewal: self development and continued education, together with personal planning to provide direction in life
- social/emotional renewal: working on the development of better relationships and genuinely being of service to others.

Covey argues that the approach of self renewal is as important for organisations as it is for individuals. He suggests that, in this case, the four **dimensions of renewal** can be:

- the physical dimension: the relevant economic factors
- the mental dimension: the way the organisation deals with its human talents
- the social/emotional dimension: the way the organisation handles its human relations
- the spiritual dimension: the contributions that the organisation makes to its environment.

In the same way as an individual needs to focus on all four dimensions, an organistion too requires a balanced, holistic approach for a healthy existence and healthy growth. If any one element is neglected then it can become a negative force retarding development.

Covey notes that these processes of renewal are ultimately the processes of continual improvement. In that regard they are also the basis of Total Quality Management and 'a key to Japan's economic ascendancy' (page 303).

Covey concludes *The seven habits of highly effective people* by relating a personal story which demonstrates the importance of communicating with others on the basis of our essential paradigms. Communication enables us to gain the opportunity to be proactive in rewriting our script, so as to change the ways in which we perceive the world: to change from the inside out.

THE CHAPTERS

(The more significant chapters are indicated by an asterisk)

Part 1

Chapter 1*   Outlines the importance of perception and discusses the concept of paradigms and paradigm shifts.

Chapter 2*   Provides an overview of the seven habits.

Part 2

Chapter 1   Discusses the first habit of being proactive.

Chapter 2*   Explores the second habit of beginning with the end in mind. This chapter includes detailed advice on the development of a personal mission statement.

Chapter 3*   Outlines the third habit of putting first things first. It includes Covey's time management matrix.

Part 3

Chapter 1*   Introduces the paradigm of interdependence and outlines the metaphor of the emotional bank account.

Chapter 2   Is about the fourth habit of win/win.

Chapter 3   Discusses the fifth habit which is based on empathic communication.

Chapter 4   Explores the concept of synergy: the sixth habit.

Part 4

Chapter 1   Is concerned with renewal, which is embodied in the 7th habit of sharpening the saw.

Chapter 2*   Relates the author's personal story of high level communication and the application of the seven habits.

Appendix A   Provides a detailed outline of the various centres that govern people's lives.

Appendix B* Outlines a simulated self-management exercise consistent with the habit of putting first things first.

8
WOMEN IN MANAGEMENT

Leonie Still – *Where to from here?:*
the managerial woman in transition
(Business and Professional Publishing 1993, 207 pages)

➡️

ABOUT THE AUTHOR

Professor Leonie Still is probably Australia's foremost researcher and authority on women in management. She has had extensive management experience in both the public and private sectors, and is currently Vice-Chancellor at Edith Cowan University in Western Australia.

Professor Still is a member of the editorial board of the international journal *Women in management review,* and has written three other texts including *Enterprising women: Australian women managers and entrepreneurs.*

THE SIGNIFICANCE OF THIS BOOK

The culmination of 10 years of research, this book includes important research findings on the progress of women in management over the last decade, and examines: women's careers; women and leadership; the barriers to success; and access to power.

Still examines success strategies for the managerial woman in the 1990s and beyond: for promotion; and for the achievement of personal and professional identity. *Where to from here?* is fundamentally a book about women's career potential.

THE AUTHOR'S BASIC ARGUMENT

Still starts by acknowledging that women managers have come a long way over the past few decades; but not far enough.

The current period we are in, Still suggests, constitutes a transition phase for women managers. On the one hand, the barriers to equality have yet to be overcome; but, on the other hand, there are major opportunities emerging within new organisational trends.

CURRENT STATUS AND OPPORTUNITIES

The ambitious woman of the 1990s is, according to Still, confronted by two opposing scenarios:

The decade for women scenario (*Still,* page 5)

In the new managerial world of team work and strategic alliances the management skills that are valued are no longer the skills of supervising, controlling and directing, but rather the softer skills of networking, team building and ethical behaviour.

Women, it is argued, are more attuned to the new styles of management and are well placed to benefit from the changes that are under way. They are more participatory, more inclined to lead by example and, over recent years, quicker to engage in self employment than are men.

The deja vu scenario (page 8)

While there might appear to be opportunities for women today, it remains the case that relatively few women make it to the top. In fact, current rates of participation by women in top management are not substantially different from rates apparent in the early 1970s.

Still points out that, in spite of the positive advances of anti-discrimination, equal employment opportunity and affirmative action policies and measures, the advance of women has been largely restricted to lower and middle management.

However one views it, though, the world *is* changing and Still believes that women can position themselves to take advantage of the new organisational trends. To do this she recommends four **strategies for advancement**:

- understand what is happening in organisations, particularly changes in the way work is undertaken and consequent changes in the role of managers
- develop a picture of the role they might play in the emerging

horizontal organisations (characterised by lateral as much as vertical movement) and revise their career aspirations accordingly

- consider radical shifts in focus during the course of their working lives in order to maximise opportunities for worthwhile and valued work within organisations
- accept that individuals now are responsible for managing their own careers and are no longer hired for life.

PROMOTING CHANGE

The remainder of *Where to from here?* is directed at promoting change in the context of an analysis of where women currently are placed.

Corporate participation

Prior to the 1990s there was significant interest and research into the position of women in the corporate labour market. Almost without exception the studies undertaken revealed that, in Australia, women worked in a relatively restricted range of occupations and industries and did not fare well when it came to gaining senior management positions.

This resulted in a spate of activity that included policy development, infrastructure support, legislation and recognition for high-achieving women in industry.

The evidence suggests, however, that there was little real change as a result of these measures. Women did not advance to the degree that was expected or hoped for. In fact, there is some evidence that the overall status of women in large organisations may have deteriorated. The glass ceiling, it seems, remains well and truly intact.

In addition, a range of studies quoted by Still reveal that men in all levels of management are still being paid more than women and are more likely to be promoted.

Still cites a number of possible explanations for all this. Reasons **why women have not achieved positions in top management** include:

- *a lack of awareness among women* of the skills and abilities they

possess and of the opportunities they could seek
- the systemic discrimination that continues to exist whereby *men are more likely to be groomed* for promotion than women
- *societal factors*: women are still less likely to apply for management positions and are still not encouraged to do so.

Not surprisingly these factors are compounded by the power relationships that tend to exist in organisations: in particular, the unwillingness of many men to share power with an emerging group of female managers.

Still outlines two alternative **strategies for increasing participation** in the male-dominated world of management:
- increase the number of women managers by reducing the number of males: a radical measure, often suggested, but not likely to be effective
- concentrate on preparing women for leadership in the new network organisations, rather than focusing on the structures of the past.

Self employment

Still reminds us that women are turning to self employment, especially the establishment of small businesses providing professional services and consulting, at a greater rate than men are. They are doing so in search of:
- autonomy
- flexibility
- the potential to succeed economically
- the chance to be creative
- the desire to work for themselves rather than someone else.

Self employment can, in Still's view, provide the opportunity for women to advance 'outside conventional organisational careers' (page 54), and hence avoid the barriers that often stand in their way. What is more, they are generally successful with a relatively low proportion reporting losses.

This is not to suggest that there is an absence of **barriers to success in self employment**. In fact Still specifically points to:
- barriers to entry: lack of confidence; insufficient access to finance; and the absence of role models or mentors

- continuation of these barriers into the operational (post-entry) phase
- personal ambivalence associated with working alone and in an insecure environment, together with the ever-present issue of managing a business and a home.

Nonetheless, women are succeeding in their own small businesses and doing better, it seems, than men are. This is, however, occurring without recognition in the broader arenas. In corporate board rooms, for example, where major decisions are being made, such facts are not well known or understood.

So these successful, capable businesswomen remain marginalised in the workforce; because self-employed women do not threaten the traditional male view of women in the corporate world and, hence, their success does little to improve their overall status and power.

Still therefore characterises the self employment trend as two steps forward and one step back.

Women managers

Women are facing a dilemma:

- if they choose to succeed by observing the 'male developed "rules" of success and promotion' (page 75), male competitors will see them as a threat and women will accuse them of selling out
- if they act in accordance with a feminist perspective they will be viewed as unsuitable for promotion by the prevailing corporate culture.

Faced with such a dilemma, most ambitious women tend either to join the dominant culture or to leave the corporate world for other employment. And those who stay follow careers that are less planned and (because they are the child bearers and rearers) less linear than those of men.

Still analyses a number of the common errors that women make in relation to their careers and concludes that the only option is for each woman to 'be proactive, not reactive, in her own career' (page 87).

She goes on to suggest that the three **most valuable strategies**

that managerial women can use to enhance their career prospects are:
- (above all) cultivating mentors to provide career support
- engaging in networking to foster professional and social contacts
- getting management training as well as specific functional or technical training.

These strategies alone are unlikely to lead to gender equity in the workplace, however. We still need on-going action on 'five levels of social organisation: societal, institutional, organisational, role and individual' (page 97).

Images of leadership

By and large, women are just not visualised in leadership positions and are not being groomed for such roles in society.

The poor representation of women in the corridors of power is a direct result of early theories about leadership and power. The traditional stereotypes of male and female traits have fostered a perception of men as decisive leaders and women as loyal followers.

Despite evidence that in many respects women provide more effective leadership than men, especially when there is a need for transformational leadership, the *loyal follower perception* still holds substantial sway. If women are to be given 'the opportunities they seek and deserve' (page 109), this gender stereotyping, amongst other negative organisational structures, will have to be challenged.

In addition to the perceptual barrier, Still identifies a number of **invisible factors at work**. These include:
- the tendency to keep moving women sideways, 'to broaden their experience', rather than vertically in organisations
- restricting the promotion of women to the more marginal areas of organisational activity
- arguments that a woman will become overloaded if she takes on additional or more important assignments.

Given all of this, Still believes that women 'will continue to be held down ... unless there is massive social and cultural change in our complex organisations' (page 123). In particular, women are unlikely to break through the glass ceiling unless there are major changes to the dominant organisational culture and the male attitudes that originally put it in place.

This is a view supported by Wendy McCarthy, AO (McCarthy, together with Imelda Roche, the Managing Director of Nutri-Metics International, is the subject of a case study in *Where to from here?*). She suggests that change over the next decade will require concerted efforts to place women in influential leadership positions whilst continuing to recruit women into all organisations.

Inevitably this will require women to establish their own personal identity. They will, however, have to do this in the face of two major, competing philosophies:

- the work mystique: where they seek to get as far as they can in their careers, irrespective of the impact on their personal lives

  or

- the feminine mystique: where the personal aspects of femininity and family assume greater importance than the pursuit of career.

The essential dilemma that arises from this in Still's view is that, irrespective of what she does or achieves, the managerial woman will remain different and also, most likely, unaccepted.

The existence of this dilemma then results in a 'questioning (of) what the work ethic and/or professional role is doing to them as women' (page 142).

Part of the problem in resolving this dilemma between professional identity and feminine identity is that only relatively few women have confronted it in the past and hence there are precious few role models in existence.

Nonetheless, Still views the issue of identity as a developmental process. Women should be encouraged to realise that, like men, they will go through various stages in their lives characterised by particular needs at any one time. They should not feel guilty, angry or resentful about choices made between family and career at various points.

This questioning of identity and, by implication, of the male managerial culture is, according to Still, a sign of maturity and development rather than of any desire to return to the past.

The issue to which Still keeps returning, however, is the dominance of the men's club in organisational culture: a dominance that continually works to limit women.

The mentor and the men's club

One successful strategy currently being used to rectify gender imbalance in the business world is the adoption by women of mentors to improve career opportunities. In the US in particular, mentoring has been identified as an important source of female career success.

Still acknowledges the value and effectiveness of mentoring as a means of gaining promotion and entry for women into management positions. She argues, however, that mentoring fails to deal with the power of the men's club once entry has been gained. Women remain unable to enter the inner circles where the organisational culture is passed on, and hence often remain marginalised.

One particularly strong element of the men's club culture that Still points to is the tendency for businessmen to operate on the basis of deals. Doing deals is, according to Still, inconsistent with the value systems of many women. Deals are so important to the managerial game, however, that women need to learn either to deal – or at least understand the dealing process – if they are to succeed in business in more than token numbers. This is a cultural change which she believes an increasing number of women is capable of making.

Still concludes *Where to from here?* by suggesting that, given the degree of organisational change in the world, there are several choices that face the managerial woman. These range from working within the traditional organisation and seeking to change it, to self employment or even to opting out altogether.

The important thing for Leonie Still is that the choice should be an informed choice.

In summary, the managerial woman of the 1990s will need to:
- ignore the backlash and focus on the gains that have been made

- reclaim the agenda by engaging in such activities as mentoring, networking and selling women's successes and achievements
- review career progress in order to determine the best direction in which to head
- target the best opportunities in areas (such as the information and service industries) where the likelihood of advancement is highest
- acquire power by learning to use the power of the positions they already hold
- acquire appropriate skills and qualifications through education and personal efforts to keep up to date
- attempt to change the culture by instituting their own change with the involvement of male colleagues and by ongoing efforts to change attitudes.

What happens next in relation to women's managerial progress is then largely 'up to them' (page 178).

THE CHAPTERS

(The more significant chapters are indicated by an asterisk)

Chapter 6   Examines the competing philosophies of 'work mys-
             tique' and 'feminine mystique' and the consequent
             struggle for the managerial woman to establish her
             own identity.

Chapter 7   Considers the continued existence of the 'men's
             club' that has dominated organisational culture, and
             the need for women to learn how to 'deal'.

Chapter 8*   Outlines a view of the future and provides advice to
             guide the choices that managerial women will have to
             make.

9
CHANGE, SHAMROCKS AND FEDERALISM

Charles Handy – *The age of unreason*
(Harvard Business School Press, 1989, 278 pages)

ABOUT THE AUTHOR

Charles Handy is visiting professor at the London Business School. He has acted as a consultant to a wide range of business and government organisations, including educational and health-care bodies. He has published several books including *The future of work* and *The making of managers*. Handy lectures throughout the world as well as providing regular commentaries for the British Broadcasting Corporation (BBC). In 1977 Handy was appointed Warden of St George's House in Windsor Castle and at the time *The age of unreason* was published he was the Chairman of the Royal Society of Arts.

THE SIGNIFICANCE OF THIS BOOK

Charles Handy is one of the gurus of modern organisation and management theory. He has written extensively and his books are widely quoted. Any Handy book is greeted with great interest and enthusiasm – especially one as innovative and thought-provoking as *The age of unreason*.

Warren Bennis, another extremely influential figure in management theory, sums up the importance of Handy's book when he writes in his foreword to it that 'Charles Handy's book is about the story of our time: change' (*Handy*, page viii).

Bennis goes on to suggest that the book 'advances our thinking with a remarkable set of new phrases' and that the book is full of 'insightful and useful ideas' (page ix). Handy's turn of phrase alone assures the book a degree of influence; and already such terms as 'the shamrock organisation' and 'the third age' are widely used both in the corporate sector and in academic tomes.

THE AUTHOR'S BASIC ARGUMENT

Handy's book is constructed on the belief that the future is not immutable and that people have the ability to shape what happens.

The book is structured into three broad sections: changing; working; and living.

CHANGING

While we all tend to accept the inevitability of change, most of us, Handy argues, prefer our change to be continuous, predictable and comfortable. Certainly events such as wars, major technological advances and significant demographic changes can disrupt the steady march forward of the status quo, but only from time to time. Handy suggests, however, that the present day circumstances are such that we have entered a new **'age of unreason'** characterised by:

1 Discontinuity

Changes are no longer part of some ongoing pattern of development. Consistent with chaos theory from the world of science, change in all facets of our lives is continually faster and less predictable – more discontinuous.

This is not something to fear: instead it presents human society with a real opportunity to advance, provided we 'learn to look for and embrace' it (page 9).

Not surprisingly, this is easier said than done. It requires a willingness to learn and to experiment, to question and take risks.

2 Small things

The smallest changes can often have the most impact. Handy illustrates this point by discussing how the seemingly small technological change associated with the development of the chimney may well have had a greater social impact than any individual war.

3 Infotech and biotech

Technology, economics and, more recently, biotechnology are especially powerful forces for change. One need look no further than the revolutionary impact that modern telecommunications is having on how (and where) work can be carried out in the 1990s.

4 Thinking upside down

A form of 'discontinuous upside-down thinking' (page 5) – thinking which challenges the existing order – will be needed to cope with the new situations in which we find ourselves. The book itself is constructed, according to Handy, on discontinuous, creative, upside-down thinking; because many of the ideas discussed represent new and different ways of looking at old and familiar problems.

There are, he says, certain **fundamental demographic numbers** that underlie our current situation and impact markedly on where we are headed. In particular he points to the fact that:

- by the 21st century less than 50 per cent of the workforce will be in conventional, full-time jobs. In addition to the unemployment and unpaid domestic work that we have tended to become used to, we are witnessing a massive growth in self employment. This necessitates a fundamental rethink of the traditional concepts of work, job and career. It also impacts on such issues as tax collection, family support and the organisation of our corporations
- an increasing proportion of the available jobs in our community require high-order intellectual rather than manual skills. This has major implications for the education system as well as for the credentials that young people are expected to acquire prior to seeking employment
- the tendency for women to re-enter the workforce will intensify. This has implications both for the way in which organisations are run and for the structure and support of the family

- old people will constitute a growing proportion of the population. This raises fundamental issues such as what they will live on, what they will actually do and, in many cases, who will take care of them. Handy focuses on this issue of the third age – the age of living that follows the ages of learning and of work – as a case where upside-down thinking is needed to produce opportunities rather than problems. For instance, he points out that many older people will be relatively well off financially and physically. They can, therefore, still contribute to society in meaningful ways through unpaid work, provided we 'rethink what jobs call for part-time wisdom and experience, and what work can be done at a distance by responsible people' (page 42).

These various demographic changes are being bolstered by a fundamental change in the nature of work and, more particularly, careers. Prior to the current generation, a young person entering the workforce could expect to work a set number of hours for a given number of weeks per year over a 35- to 45-year period. This is no longer the case. Today, people are working more intensively but over fewer years; they are leaving and reentering the workforce with greater regularity; and they are retiring earlier to pursue other interests or career options.

These changes in the nature of work and career are a consequence of the trend away from labour-intensive manufacturing and towards knowledge-based organisations and the provision of services. Each of the changes contributes to the development of new forms of organisation as well as to new ways of working and living.

A focus on such dramatic developments as these might encourage the view that some sort of crisis is necessary for change to occur. Handy is quick to point out, however, that change is also something that we can choose to manage for ourselves, provided we are prepared to engage in a process of continual learning – because those who do constantly seek to learn are the ones who see the real opportunities in our ever-changing world.

Since learning is so central to coping with change, Handy concludes the first section of his book with an outline of a theory

of learning. More specifically, he views learning in terms of a
continually turning wheel – **'life's special treadmill'** (page 58) –
which involves:

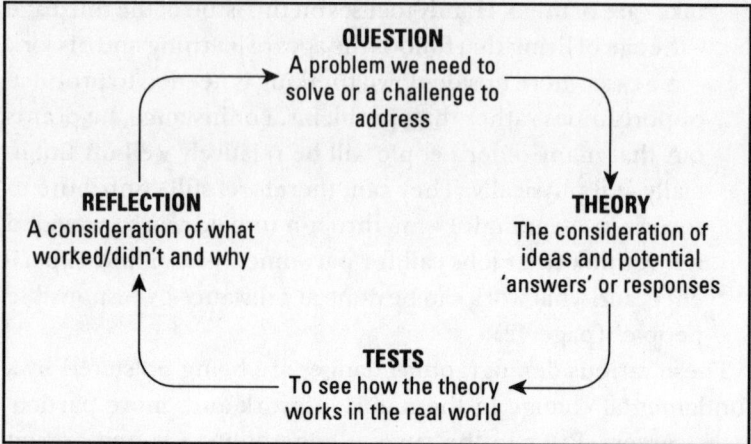

QUESTION
A problem we need to
solve or a challenge to
address

REFLECTION
A consideration of what
worked/didn't and why

THEORY
The consideration of
ideas and potential
'answers' or responses

TESTS
To see how the theory
works in the real world

Of course many people get stuck in one or other of the spokes
of the wheel so it ceases to turn and learning fails to occur. They
succumb to particular **blocks to the wheel of learning**, the most
notable being:

- the 'they' syndrome: where people either refuse, or fail to
  take, responsibility for their own lives, waiting instead for the
  unnamed they to do it for them
- futility/humility: where people do not sufficiently believe in
  themselves to push issues or seek answers to difficult questions, with the result that learning stops
- the theft of purposes: where goals are imposed on people
  rather than being negotiated with them; and where people
  then effectively lose their desire to learn
- the missing forgiveness: in which mistakes are recorded using
  appraisal and assessment processes, thereby producing an
  unwillingness to try an idea or take a risk.

There are, however, some **lubricants for the wheel of learning**.
The three that Handy nominates are:

- a proper selfishness: where people take responsibility for
  themselves, are clear about their desired future and genuinely want it, and then believe that they can achieve it

- a way of reframing: seeing things from different perspectives so as to identify new possibilities and options
- a negative capability: people's capacity to live with uncertainty, ambiguity and failure, without which they are less likely to take the risks that are required to really learn and change.

Handy concludes this section on change by providing four exercises (pages 77-80) designed to lubricate the all important process of ongoing learning.

WORKING

Handy introduces the second section of his book with **three vignettes of discontinuous change** occurring in relation to work:

- a retired friend who has established his own enterprise that enables him to continue earning while increasingly mixing business with pleasure
- his own children, in their twenties, who engage in jobs that did not exist a generation ago and who anticipate changing jobs many times over the course of their working lives
- a young unemployed man he heard interviewed on the radio who has no qualifications and who sees no future for himself in society.

He argues that we are in a **chicken-and-egg situation** where:

- the changes occurring in the world of work are a consequence of the changes within the organisations

and yet at the same time

- the organisations are having to adapt to new ways of doing work.

Modern organisations are increasingly focused on outputs and effectiveness. There is increased pressure for results. This, together with the trend towards knowledge-based production, has fundamentally changed organisational requirements for personnel and hence the way in which employees are managed. These changes in personnel requirements and personnel management are represented in Handy's three organisational models: the shamrock organisation; federalism; and the triple I organisation. These three interrelated concepts can be explained as follows:

The shamrock organisation

The shamrock is, of course, the three-leaf clover, Ireland's national emblem. Handy uses this symbol to represent his picture of the organisation that is made up of three separate groups of employees – core workers, contractors and the flexible labour force – each of which is organised, managed and remunerated quite differently:

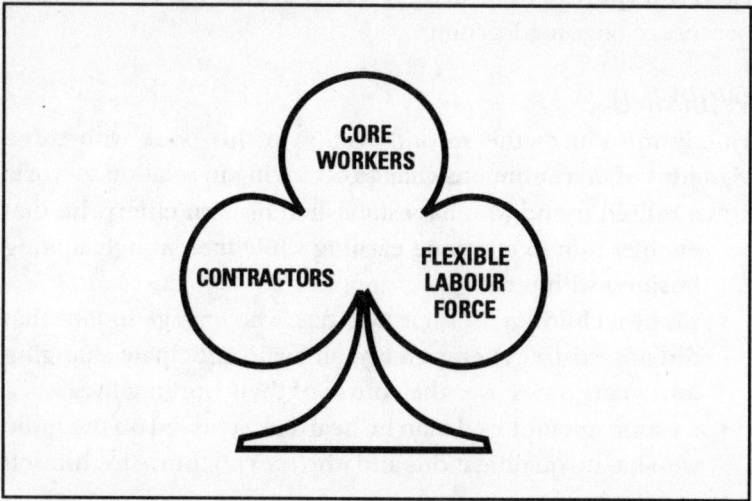

- The core workers, consisting of the talented, dedicated professionals, are highly paid and work very long hours. They 'own the organisational knowledge which distinguishes that organisation from its counterparts' (page 90). Because this core is very costly, it is a component which the organisation constantly seeks to shrink; turning instead to the second leaf of the shamrock, the contractors.
- The contractors are the specialists who carry out work considered nonessential by the core workers: work that the organisation itself prefers to be done by someone else. Such work can range from cleaning to work requiring high-level expertise.
- The flexible labour force is made up of the part-time and temporary workers who work (or don't work) according to the peaks and troughs in customer demand.

(Handy also points to a possible fourth leaf to account for the situation where customers themselves undertake the work. This is manifest in the trend towards self service. Since this is unpaid work, however, it is not explored in any depth.)

While the shamrock organisation is based on sound economics, it does create difficulties for management who are now dealing with three workforces rather than one, each requiring a different style of management:

- the highly-qualified, hard-working and committed core expect to be treated as equals – partners rather than subordinates – whose remuneration largely relates to their performance
- the contracted group are paid solely for the work they do. The employing organisation is concerned with the results they produce rather than the means adopted, and their commitment is effectively bought through the rewards offered for the contracts undertaken
- the flexible labour force includes many people who have no desire to work full time, including self-employed people with a portfolio of jobs. They are committed to a task, and possibly to a work group, but they have no strong commitment to either the organisation itself or to the concept of a career for themselves. Since they constitute a significant component of the organisation's workforce, it is important to ensure that they are not neglected and treated purely as casual labour. When they are treated that way their performance suffers.

Technological developments, especially telecommunications, have strengthened the shamrock organisation because they allow people to work from their homes or, in fact, from almost anywhere.

The shamrock structure is useful when there is no need to operate only with full-time employees. It does, however, present a number of quite specific challenges. For instance: organising meetings that involve non-core workers; clearly identifying the types of activities and employees that belong in the core; and selecting the right people for the various component parts of the organisation.

The federal organisation

Handy's federal organisation is an attempt to combine autonomy with cooperation by uniting individual groups around a common mission and identity.

Federalism is not just decentralisation, where the all-powerful centre delegates particular responsibilities to the parts. In some respects it is the exact opposite: the parts of a federation operate with a great deal of autonomy and the centre merely sets the overall direction, coordinating activities and exploiting potential economies of scale.

It is a logical extension of the shamrock model, but one in which the organisational core itself is contracted out.

Federalism is, according to Handy, 'a concept devised to **make things big while keeping them small**' (page 122). This requires:

- a centre that thinks about the bigger picture and makes the big decisions in consultation with the outlying parts of the organisation
- leadership of the sort that is concerned with ideas and the strategic direction of the organisation, as described also by Jan Carlzon in *Moments of truth*.
- 'subsidiarity', which Handy describes as the situation where the centre willingly gives away power because it trusts those in the outlying parts to make the correct decisions in the circumstances they confront
- the development of 'inverted doughnut' jobs: where the solid centre consists of work that is strictly defined by the organisation, whereas the surrounding hole is where the employee has both responsibility and the freedom to act. The empty space of the inverted doughnut (bounded only by the limits of the individual's discretion to make decisions and act) is the area where the employee can demonstrate initiative and take a risk.

The combination of these factors requires a totally new **approach to management** whereby management:

- is based on results, not means

- accepts that mistakes will be made and that they are to be forgiven and learnt from
- aims to promote learning within the organisation
- expects uncertainty
- promotes trust rather than control.

In a word, management through true leadership.

The triple I organisation

It is not enough for a modern organisation to be federal: it has also to be smart, because wealth today derives from the application of knowledge. The triple I referred to by Handy encompasses intelligence, information and ideas, today's sources of value added.

In the triple I organisation people are paid to think and to do, and management is based on persuasion and consent rather than command. Individual and group work is supported by the use of smart machines such as personal computers and robots.

One of the most significant aspects of the triple I approach is, in Handy's view, that each of the members of the professional core will not only possess their own area of expertise, but will also have to be a manager. In the course of their work everyone will be involved in managing projects, people and money. They will, therefore, constantly need to upgrade their skills both through their own efforts and as a consequence of the organisation's endeavour to be a real learning organisation.

LIVING

As organisations and the nature of work change, so must our whole way of life. Handy suggests that we are in an era where, for the very first time, we have the opportunity to shape our work to suit our lives, rather than the other way around. This requires, however, that we first redefine the term 'work' so that it is no longer synonymous with having a paid job. Rather, work should be seen as a major opportunity to gain meaning in our lives and to contribute to society. 'Work is the purpose of life'. It 'gives us a pattern or structure for our days and a chance to meet new people' (page 181).

Portfolios

Handy suggests that we adopt the concept of portfolios: a way of describing how the various pieces of the work we do fit together in a balanced and coherent way. There are, he argues, five types of work that could be incorporated in our **balanced work portfolios**. The first two types are paid, while the latter three are instances of free work:

- wage and salary work: where we are paid for the time we give
- fee work: similar to wage and salary work except that the payment relates to results achieved rather than to time spent on the task
- homework: all the activities that occur in the home
- gift work: the work done outside of the home for no fee
- study work: including training, learning and reading.

As our careers become progressively shorter, especially if we are working in a professional core, we will increasingly seek fulfilment in all five categories and not merely in a paid, full-time job. In addition, more and more of us will gain our income from a portfolio of paid activities, much as many small businesses have always done.

We will increasingly be compelled to adopt a portfolio approach to life as a whole. Handy shows how the approach is as applicable to, say, marriage as it is to employment.

Reinventing education

Having considered the concept of portfolio lives, Handy explores the 'reinvention' (page 168) of education in some depth. With learning as the key to change, 'education has to become the single most important investment that any person can make in their own destiny' (page 211). For education to change sufficiently, Handy suggests that:

- education and learning will become a lifelong activity, not something that stops at age 18
- schools, like all organisations, will be affected by the principles that underpin the shamrock organisation and federalism
- organisations will increasingly need to become 'learning

organisations': where the organisation itself learns while also encouraging all of its people to learn.

An important aspect of learning organisations is that they *care* for the individual. An attitude of caring is, according to Handy, essential for a climate of trust to develop within the organisation: the sort of trust which supports federalism and encourages experimentation and risk taking.

Handy concludes his book by suggesting that the changes in work that he describes are profound: so profound that they will require government to rethink and reframe in order to meet the challenges occasioned by discontinuity. They will:

- (like private sector corporations) contract out core activities
- collect taxes differently
- find new ways to influence the economy as a whole.

All of this occasions a need, in Handy's terms, for some upside-down thinking: the sort of thinking that could see the shamrock organisation and federalism extending to the public sector; thinking that discounts no idea on the basis that it appears unreasonable but instead encourages new ways of seeing in order to improve our social order.

THE CHAPTERS

(The more significant chapters are indicated by an asterisk)

Chapter 1*	Presents the basic argument about discontinuous change and the need for upside-down thinking.
Chapter 2	Outlines the fundamental demographic and economic changes that are leading to new ways of organising, working and living.
Chapter 3*	Provides a theory of learning and an outline of the blockages to and lubricants for the wheel of learning and change.
Chapter 4*	Explains the concept of the 'shamrock organisation'.
Chapter 5*	Defines the 'federal organisation' and the concept of federalism.
Chapter 6*	Explores the importance of intelligence, information and ideas for adding value in modern organisations.

Chapter 7   Outlines the concept of 'portfolios' and discusses it
              with particular reference to our work and our home
              life.
Chapter 8   Advocates the 'reinvention' of education with a par-
              ticular focus on shamrock schools, upside-down
              schools and learning organisations.
Chapter 9   Considers the impact of various discontinuities on
              the public sector and society, and examines the need
              for more upside-down thinking.

10
THE SOCIETY OF KNOWLEDGE AND ORGANISATIONS

Peter Drucker – *Post-capitalist society*
(Butterworth-Heinemann, 1993, 204 pages)

ABOUT THE AUTHOR

Peter Drucker has variously been a newspaper correspondent, an economist for an international bank, a management consultant and a university professor. He is the author of numerous books including *Managing for the future, Managing for results, The effective executive* and *Managing in turbulent times,* and he is currently the Clarke Professor of Social Science at the Claremont Graduate School in California.

THE SIGNIFICANCE OF THIS BOOK

Peter Drucker is, along with Charles Handy, one of the most influential thinkers and mentors in modern management. In fact, the magazine *Business Week* has called him 'the most enduring management thinker of our time' (cover note).

Thus, any book that Drucker writes tends to be greeted with great interest and accorded significance by the human resources profession.

In *Post-capitalist society* Peter Drucker has moved beyond mere management theory to a discussion of the changes that are currently impacting on politics, economics and the global society in which we live. It is a book where he endeavours to analyse current trends so as to assess, if not predict, what the future may hold and identify the opportunities that await us.

The book describes the big picture in which management

theories are developed and enacted. It is designed to chart the major transformations that the late twentieth century society is experiencing and to draw out the implications for individuals and organisations.

Given that some parts of the book are deeply ideological, it could well be described as an outline of Peter Drucker's *credo*.

THE AUTHOR'S BASIC ARGUMENT

Drucker introduces his book by arguing that, once every few centuries, western society undergoes a major transformation which leads to the creation of a whole new way of life: a change so significant that people 'cannot even imagine the world ... into which their own parents were born' (*Drucker*, page 1).

The creation of post-capitalist society in the late twentieth century is, according to Drucker, a transformation of this order; with the interesting additional dimension that, on this occasion, the whole world is involved, but in an increasingly western way.

While Drucker is quick to point out that we cannot know what the future may hold, he does argue that some **aspects of the emerging society** are clear; in particular, that:

- it will resemble neither the capitalist nor the socialist societies of the past: the traditional capitalist-industrial proletariat division no longer holds good because of the emergence of a vast group of knowledge and service workers; and individual company owners are increasingly giving way to professional managers and large institutional funds

- knowledge will be the major resource: knowledge work has become the prime source of value added and knowledge workers are increasingly becoming society's most significant economic and social grouping

- it will be a society of organisations and networks: while knowledge workers generally operate in organisations of one form or another, these often take the form of loose and impermanent networks formed to undertake particular tasks

- the total dominance of nation states will soften and give way to global connections and local (regional and tribal) structures for decision making. Nation states will not disappear, but government functions increasingly will be shared across national boundaries and with various forms of local authority.

With this as his background, Drucker proceeds to a more detailed analysis of society's transformation under the three headings of society, polity and knowledge.

SOCIETY

The development of capitalism from the time of the Industrial Revolution has been associated with a radical change in the way that knowledge in society is perceived. In particular there has been a shift from a conception of knowledge as purely for greater understanding and self-development to a view of knowledge as also being *useful,* a view which has underpinned the development and spread of skills and technology.

While knowledge is still seen as a personal good, it also has come to be viewed as a public resource.

This fundamental shift in thinking has occasioned, according to Drucker, a series of **revolutions that underpin modern capitalism**; specifically:

- the Industrial Revolution (from about 1700 onwards) which saw the emergence of
    - technology, where knowledge is applied to tools, processes and products
    - the first technological schools
    - books (such as *The encyclopedie*) that outlined the mysteries of the crafts for all who sought to know them.

    With these changes, 'production almost overnight moved from being craft-based to being technology-based' (page 26).
- the 'productivity revolution' (from about 1880) which saw knowledge applied to work itself. Starting with the work of Frederick Winslow Taylor, an attempt was made to analyse and organise work so that it could be performed more productively. The productivity explosion that followed led to rapid economic development and a rising standard of living in the western world.
- the 'management revolution', which is seeing knowledge

applied not only to tools, processes, products and human work, but also to knowledge itself. In the management revolution non-manual rather than manual workers are the major contributors to value added and the task of management is to ensure that knowledge is applied as effectively as possible to produce the results that are sought. This reflects the fact that knowledge is now the most important factor of production.

As an interesting consequence of the management revolution, where work is valued for what it can do or produce, knowledge is becoming increasingly specialised; which leads Drucker to write of 'knowledges' rather than just knowledge.

Organisations are, like knowledge, becoming increasingly specialised too: they have become groups of 'specialists working together on a common task' (page 43).

Today's society is, according to Drucker, a **society of organisations**, because:

- virtually all social tasks are undertaken by organisations
- organisations are the means by which separate and highly specialised knowledges can be joined together to work productively

The symphony orchestra provides a good analogy:

- the combined talents of many highly specialised musicians all focus on a common task
- the product comes from the orchestra as a whole, rather than from any individuals
- success depends upon a high quality performance from each and every player.

For the orchestra or any organisation to **perform effectively**, it is necessary that:

- both the mission and the immediate task are abundantly clear to everyone
- the results are clearly specified
- the performance is assessed against a clear set of goals and objectives
- the organisation is managed: because there needs to be someone who accepts responsibility for making decisions and for achieving results.

In a knowledge organisation this management cannot be coercive, but rather will involve directing: uniting people around the mission and the strategies for pursuing it. It also will involve the management of change in order to seek improvement continually, to develop new ways of doing things and to promote innovation.

Having considered the role of organisations in post-capitalist society, Drucker moves on to a discussion of the **role of labour and capital** (the traditional factors of production) in an age where knowledge is the fundamental resource. What we will see, he suggests, is:

- the disappearance of labour as an asset. Blue-collar employment is shrinking throughout the western world. Some countries, notably Japan, are even exporting their manufacturing jobs to the cheaper workers of the developing countries. This enables them to concentrate instead on the high value-added, knowledge-based industries. The major employment demands over coming years will be for knowledge workers or technicians who have a high level of formal education and an ability to learn throughout their lives. This applies as much to manufacturing as to any other sector, since knowledge is increasingly being applied to all of the processes of production.

- 'capitalism without capitalists' (page 61). Some of today's biggest holders of financial assets are superannuation or pension funds; and the ageing of the population will only consolidate this trend. The major sources of future investment will be institutional funds run by managers rather than by very wealthy capitalists. Since these funds consist of the deferred earnings of millions of employees, we are likely to see the emergence of new forms of governance, management and accountability focused on longer-term rather than short-term results.

Knowledge and service workers constitute an increasing proportion of the modern workforce and must become the prime focus of organisations and society. If their productivity is to be improved, Drucker suggests that it will first be necessary to:

- define their performance by specifying the results to be
  achieved
- establish the appropriate team for carrying out the work
- enable workers to concentrate on the work by eliminating
  any activities that do not contribute to achieving the expected results
- turn to the workers themselves
  - tapping into their knowledge and ideas
  - giving them responsibility for their own performance
  - empowering them to control their own work
  - promoting continuous learning in and on the job.

All of this requires, however, that our existing organisations
undergo substantial (if not fundamental) restructuring. In particular, organisations will become flatter and many of the support
activities will be outsourced to specialist, more productive contractors.

Drucker concludes his discussion of society by arguing that,
being the age of the organisation, post-capitalist society will have
a **'responsibility-based organisation'** as its key structure; an organisation that:

- exercises social responsibility
- does not exceed the legitimate limits of its competence and
  its function in society
- consists of employees who accept responsibility for the work
  of the organisation, their own contribution to that work and
  the way in which they behave.

POLITY

The changes occurring in our political systems and structures
(our 'polity') are, according to Drucker, as significant as the
societal changes to which he has already referred.

In particular he argues that since World War 2 we have seen the
nation state (established originally to defend civil society) transformed into a more interventionist **'megastate'** characterised as:

- 'the nanny state': providing services, including welfare, finan-
  ced from tax revenue
- 'the fiscal state': exerting political influence on the economic

direction of society by redistributing income and/or managing the state of the economy
or
- 'the cold war state': orienting much of its economy towards
  significant levels of arms production for defence purposes.

Drucker argues that the megastate has demonstrably failed to
work, citing such examples as: the western world's inability to
manage its economies; and the collapse of eastern European
communism. In many instances this failure, he says, results from
the tendency of politicians to make decisions aimed at buying
votes rather than at doing the right thing: the 'pork barrel state'.
But above all, Drucker sees the failure of the megastate as flowing
from the tendency that governments have of trying to do everything rather than setting the basic parameters and then monitor-
ing performance: what Osborne and Gaebler would call 'rowing
rather than steering'.

The failure of the megastate does not, however, signal a return
to the nation states of the past. There are forces at work which
make this impossible; specifically:

- 'transnationalism': whereby individual states are unable to
  control their own destiny because the movement of money
  and the spread of information have effectively been globalised.
  Modern responses to this include:
    - transnational organisations such as the European Com-
      munity
    - transnational action such as the UN action against Iraq.
  These responses have further impacted on the traditional
  sovereignty of nations.
- 'regionalism': where regional governing bodies take over
  major areas of activity at the expense of national governments. There are good examples of this in the area of trade:
    - the North American Free Trade Association (NAFTA)
    - the Asia Pacific Economic Community (APEC).
  (Drucker suggests that one reason for these two trends is
  that 'the knowledge economy requires…economic units that
  are substantially *larger* than even a fair-sized national state'
  (page 137).)

- 'tribalism': a focus on diversity rather than unity within a country. Sometimes this tribalism becomes utterly danger-ous, as is the case in the former state of Yugoslavia. Tribalism arises from the fact that bigness is no longer required for access to money or information, and can even threaten the continued viability of some nation states.

As people and groups strive for a sense of community in a transnational world, they tend to seek roots to which they can effectively graft themselves.

These three tendencies (transnationalism, regionalism and tribalism) are occurring in the context of 'the work of govern-ment still ... (needing to) ... go on' (page 141). Thus, in Drucker's view, one of the most urgent political tasks the world faces is **to improve the performance of governments** in the emerging post-capitalist society. This, he argues, will require:

- abandoning those things that are not working
- focusing attention on those things that are working and seeking to extend them
- analysing activities which are only partially successful so as to apply the previous two requirements to them.

Drucker then discusses this approach to turning around gov-ernment performance with specific reference to the issues of military aid and economic policy. He also considers the imple-mentation of social programs by the nanny state and concludes that, while government has generally achieved relatively little in this sphere, autonomous community organisations have often been very successful. This leads him to propose, in the post-capitalist polity, a 'new Social Sector – both to satisfy social needs and to restore meaningful citizenship and community' (pages 150-1).

Social needs will, in Drucker's view, grow in relation to both charity and community development. He argues, however, that these are both things that are better contracted out than under-taken by government; because community organisations do them better, while also promoting a degree of meaningful citizenship.

Participation in the social sector can also provide individuals in society with meaningful relationships and activity outside of their work and a chance to contribute something to their community that extends beyond their specific area of (working) expertise. Thus, the importance of the social, volunteer sector is not merely that it is needed for the provision of certain services, but also that it provides a sense of community and promotes active citizenship for community members.

KNOWLEDGE

Post-capitalism, like capitalism before it, is a market-based economy. What is new, however, is that the sources of wealth in today's market are knowledge and information. Returns on the traditional factors of production are, on the other hand, declining.

Knowledge as a resource is an expensive commodity. Our education systems, our on-the-job training and our research and development all require a major investment of community funds. Thus, there is a growing interest in the productivity of knowledge and how it can be enhanced.

Drucker is clear in his view that this cannot be achieved through central planning and direction as these tend to stifle creativity and innovation. Rather, decentralisation and diversity must be the basis of any systematic attempts to **improve the productivity of knowledge**. Achieving this is, in Drucker's view, a management responsibility. It involves:

- aiming high
- seeking to make continuous step-by-step improvements
- providing a clear focus for the application of knowledge
- seizing on opportunities which relate to the organisation's knowledge-based strengths
- balancing the need for short-term results with the need to take time to raise the productivity of knowledge.

Since the foundations of a knowledge-based society are laid in our schools, Drucker follows up his discussion of the productivity of knowledge with a chapter on the 'accountable school' (page 177).

Drucker acknowledges that no-one can definitively state what the **school of the post-capitalist knowledge society** should be like;

but he does suggest that there are certain specifications that can be identified. The school will need to:

- provide high-level universal literacy: encompassing numeracy, a basic understanding of science/technology, contact with another language, skill in operating in a team environment
- promote a passion for learning and a commitment to life-long learning
- provide access for all, including adults seeking either to return to school or advance their formal education
- address both content (specific knowledge) and process
- recognise that schooling is only one source of education in society; and that schools will increasingly form partnerships with other education and training providers.

Drucker is convinced that schools, given their importance in the knowledge society and the level of resources they attract, will increasingly be called to account for their bottom line: they will have to clearly specify the results they are seeking and then achieve those results.

Since educated people are at the centre of the knowledge society, Drucker concludes his discussion of knowledge, and indeed his book, with a consideration of what constitutes **the educated person**. True to the rest of *Post-capitalist society*, he suggests that the educated person is someone who:

- can live in a global world: a westernised world that is experiencing a revival of tribalism
- can operate in a world of organisations, living and working both as the 'intellectual who focuses on words and ideas' and as the 'manager who focuses on people and work' (page 195)
- can combine highly specialised knowledge with an understanding of the other knowledges that impact (or may impact) on it.

THE CHAPTERS

(The more significant chapters are indicated by an asterisk)

Introduction* Discusses the transformation of society into a post-capitalist state, in particular as a consequence of the development of a knowledge-based society.

Chapter 1*		Traces the development of the knowledge society and includes a discussion of what knowledge means in the modern world.

Chapter 2*		Considers what happens to organisations in society when knowledge is the fundamental resource.

Chapter 3		Analyses the roles of labour and capital, the traditional factors of production, in post-capitalism, and considers what this means for the management of corporations.

Chapter 4*		Discusses some of the new sources of productivity such as working in teams, organisational restructuring and the contracting out of non-core functions.

Chapter 5		Looks at the social responsibilities of organisations in post-capitalist society.

Chapter 6		Charts the emergence of the 'megastate' and the consequent decline in significance of nation states.

Chapter 7		Discusses the globalisation of money and information, and the trend to increased regionalisation and tribalism around the world, and shows how these trends preclude a return to the nation state of the past.

Chapter 8		Examines some areas where government performance can be markedly improved, in Drucker's view.

Chapter 9		Canvasses the need for a new social sector based on community rather than government, and includes a discussion of the 'volunteer as citizen' in post-capitalist society.

Chapter 10		Considers the productivity of knowledge and the implications this has for management in the modern world.

Chapter 11		Outlines the concept of the 'accountable school' in the context of a discussion of what constitutes learning in the knowledge society.

Chapter 12		Advances a view of the educated person in the knowledge society.